The Right Price
For Your Business

The Right Price for Your Business

Other Books by Morris A. Nunes

Operational Cash Flow Management & Control (Prentice-Hall, Inc., 1982)

The Property Maintenance Logbook (with William Chargar; Prentice-Hall, Inc., 1985)

Balance Sheet Management (John Wiley & Sons, 1987)

The Right Price
For Your Business

Morris A. Nunes

WILEY

John Wiley & Sons
New York • Chichester • Brisbane • Toronto • Singapore

Copyright © 1988 by John Wiley & Sons, Inc.

Library of Congress Cataloging in Publication Data:

Nunes, Morris A., 1949–
   The right price for your business.
     p. cm.
   Bibliography: p.
   Includes index.
   ISBN 0-471-62562-0
   1. Business enterprises, Sale of. 2. Business enterprises—
Purchasing. I. Title.

HD 1393.25.N86 1988
658.1'6—dc19   88-15514
                                             CIP

Printed in the United States of America

10 9 8 7 6 5 4 3 2 1

To my Father,

Myron A. Nunes

(1925–1985)

He taught me the values that really matter

Preface

For most business owners, their company is the keystone of their wealth. But it is often much more than just a business enterprise. It is also an occupation, a livelihood, a source of pride—even an identity.

With so much at stake, it is often difficult for owners and would-be owners to evaluate dispassionately. Many owners recognize the wisdom of obtaining assistance in making purchase and sales decisions. Appraisers, accountants, lawyers, investment bankers, business brokers, commercial bankers, and even insurance agents have been known to participate in putting a deal together.

It is for all of them—sellers, buyers, and their advisors—that this book is written.

What it offers is a new, yet classical, approach to the subject of business pricing. The classical approach is a combination of investment analysis and financial analysis. What is new is the combination of the two—both the fact and method of combination—in the process of finding a realistic price for a business enterprise.

The investment analysis is not unlike that performed by Wall Street securities analysts in evaluating and predicting stock prices. As a former securities analyst myself, I am confident those methods have enormous, even obvious, applicability to the subject.

The financial analysis is not unlike the analysis that controllers, treasurers, and chief financial officers routinely perform and rely on in making equipment purchase and operational financing decisions. As a former corporate controller, I have no doubt the same financial principles attend.

It is worth noting that a natural consequence of pursuing this approach is automatic investigation of all the standard appraisal methods. These methods are part of the classical approach, but what is new is that the investigation relates each of them to the central thesis of the combination approach to business pricing.

That central thesis in the development of this combination approach is that value and price are ultimately related to the rewards ownership will provide. Quantify and qualify the rewards, and it is not too hard to decide how much one should pay to obtain them. Value for owners is thus derived from earning a real return above the cost of capital employed. Price, then, must be a function of the potential return and the applicable cost of capital, all adjusted for risk.

The core of that analysis is numerical and borrows heavily from the financial analyst's repertoire. But with a transaction so rich in nonfinancial attributes and so prone to the panoply of risks prevalent and imaginable in today's business world, a heavy dose of market savvy and business judgment is essential. Here the securities analyst's arsenal provides a way to make sense of the jumble of information about and crosscurrents involving the business and its environment.

The litmus test of a price is the reaction of the marketplace. But the marketplace and its players rarely react solely on the basis of statistics. If numerical precision were the sole prerequisite, the only advisor an owner would need would be a computer hard-wired for the predetermined business math program.

The marketplace is influenced by much more than numbers, and what this book also contains are many points of discussion to help "sell" a price as the right one, whether the price is bid or asked. Understanding how a price is constructed, what foundations it rests on, what returns it anticipates, what capital costs it intuits, and what risks it apprehends provides the greatest flexibility in making a deal fly. Such understanding permits a transactor to propose terms and conditions that fit into and build on the rationale for a price.

Closely related are the hints and ideas sprinkled throughout the book to help make the post-transaction business a success. With so many sales financed (at least in part) by sellers, former owners have as great a stake as new owners in seeing the business prosper.

Along the same lines, the combination approach—focusing as it does on returns, capital costs, and risks—offers a ready-made framework for developing a goal-oriented post-transaction business plan. This approach inherently accepts the premise that business price is not a fleeting value in momentary isolation, but is and will be the key determinant for the future of the business. The returns it assumes must be realized to justify the price. The cost of capital it postulates must be held in check to justify the price. The risks it appreciates must be countered to justify the price.

It is just a short journey from the pricing framework to an operational business and financial plan. The initial signposts are in this book. The road is mapped out in additional detail in my companion book, *Balance Sheet Management* (New York: John Wiley & Sons, Inc., 1987) which also may be of interest to business owners and advisors as an aid in ongoing business management.

The task of owning and growing a business is a noble undertaking. Whether it is a task accomplished by a seller or hungered for by a buyer, the single best measure of its scope is the price of the business itself.

It is my fondest hope as author that this book will help everyone involved in every transaction draw a lasting measure of satisfaction from the noble undertaking.

MORRIS A. NUNES

Falls Church, Virginia
September, 1988

Acknowledgments

My sincere thanks to:

Dr. Thomas G. Martin of Georgetown University Hospital for the use of his home as a writer's sanctuary.

The members of the Washington Independent Writer's Northern Virginia Non-Fiction Subgroup for stylistic comments, suggestions, and encouragement: Janet Auten, Scott Brayton, Cecelia Cassidy, Jack Harrison, Robbie Kaplan, John Kelly, Joan Lisante, Paula Odin, Stephanie Overman, Tom Robinson, Ellen Ryan, George Soules, Judith Sullivan, and, especially, Judith Kelly.

Hewlett-Packard Corporation for inventing the HP-67 programmable calculator, which saved me countless hours in calculations.

To all those friends who encouraged me: Connie Badger, Pris Bornmann, Nancy Haile, John Grasser, Susan Fattig, Mark Bayer, Vicki Schwartz, and Joe & Jeri Gargiulo.

My four-year-old son, Ryan, for his help in photocopying, for his enthusiasm, and for understanding far beyond his years.

Most especially my wife, Janie, for her great patience and support throughout these efforts.

M.A.N.

Contents

About the Author

Morris A. Nunes is an attorney and financial consultant in suburban Washington, D.C. He has advised many buyers and sellers of businesses from initial negotiations to completed transactions.

A graduate of the University of Pennsylvania and its Wharton School of Business, he holds degrees in finance and accounting. He spent several years in controllership positions before obtaining a law degree from Georgetown University.

He is the author of *Balance Sheet Management* (Wiley, 1987), co-author of "The Property Maintenance Logbook," and has written articles for the American Management Association's *Management Review, Public Utilities*

Fortnightly, Commercial Construction News, The Editorial Eye and many other publications. He has also written minicomputer financial analysis programs published by Hewlett-Packard Co.

Mr. Nunes has taught finance and tax courses in college and continuing education programs and is a frequent speaker to business and professional groups. He produces and hosts a weekly cable television program on legal subjects and holds a patent on a food storage invention.

Mr. Nunes is admitted to the Virginia, District of Columbia, and Federal bars and is licensed before several appellate courts, including the U.S. Tax Court and the U.S. Supreme Court.

An avid racquet sportsman, he lives with his wife of 18 years, Janie, their son, Ryan, and their Yorkie, Valentino, in Northern Virginia.

List of Illustrations

The Right Price
For Your Business

Introduction

Mutual advantage is the underpinning of all economic activity. Whether one sells a candy bar or a candy business, the concept of mutual advantage predominates every transaction. Unless each side believes it is coming out ahead, no deal will be made. While a business sale has some zero-sum attributes, as do most give-and-take economic transfers, buyers and sellers should not be adversaries. Wary cooperation is the ticket to realizing the advantage each must see to go forward with a purchase and sale.

This book explores the procedures and techniques for determining the best price to make the most of a business sale transaction—from both points of view. Considering the buyer and seller (the transactors) together clarifies the goals and perspectives of both. The position of each is more understandable when seen against the backdrop of its counterpart.

Price determines the bottom line. The price of a business cannot be set in a vacuum. A price, any price, if it is to be meaningful at all, must appear realistic to both sides. The price set by one side has little meaning unless it is accepted by the other side. If it is not accepted, its usefulness is limited to being a guidepost on the road to another offer price.

The seller would like a price approaching infinity. The buyer would love to buy the business for nothing. We can imagine those two extremes as opposite ends of a dollar scale. The two parties must move along the scale, away from those unrealistic extreme desires and toward each other, if a meeting of the minds is to take place. Only then can they accomplish what they set out for—a deal. Curiously, either party will attain the greatest theoretical benefit by moving along the dollar scale in the *opposite* direction from the desires of the counterpart; but if either tries to move too far, neither benefits for the transaction will not occur.

These axioms are well known but often overlooked because they are so simple, even obvious. It is necessary to restate them because they point up the dilemma of any party to an offer. Whether making an offer or trying to decide if it's acceptable, "How high or how low do you go?" The dilemma suggests its own solution, the fundamental touchstone of a transaction:

VALUE

A business, just like any other asset, will have a specific value at any particular moment for one or a combination of four straightforward reasons:

1. Because the asset will produce a stream of income (potentially including operating savings and/or tax savings) for the owner;
2. Because the asset will have a greater value in the future than it costs today;
3. Because the asset can serve as a storehouse of value;
4. Because the owner will derive emotional satisfaction or psychic gratification from the asset or from the fact of his or her ownership of it.

The very concept of a business value is elusive, much like a phantom. We know the business has a value, but it's always changing, always ahead of us, even though we intend to place a value on a business now, in the present tense. The phantom effect arises, though, because the value comes not so much from today's income, today's net worth, or today's activity, but because of what prospects for income, net worth, and activity the same business will have tomorrow. Then, as the future arrives and becomes the past, we are already focused on the next future, repredicting prospects and recalculating a value.

Without a future, the business is essentially worthless. Even the value the business would have if it were just liquidated is determined largely by the aggregate values of the assets the business has for sale in liquidation. Those assets themselves will have individual values only, again, because someone has a future use or desire for them. A defunct business whose only asset is an inventory of uncoated asbestos ceiling tiles will be worthless (or even a negative number as there may be a cost to dispose of what is considered a low-level hazardous waste product).

So to determine a value for purposes of offering or accepting a price, one must be a little bit the clairvoyant because to see a value is to see the future. To realize a gain on that value in a transaction, by achieving a purchase below the value as buyer or making a sale above the value as seller, is to seize the future.

To target a *single* value for all kinds of transactions is not uncommon. However, a single value is also not optimal, because a business may simultaneously have more than one value, depending at any one time upon who is seeking the value and for what purpose.

With value as a reference point, establishing a price tailored to a special goal is the way to maximize the future by consciously promoting the best transaction outcome. Using value to set a price goal will have potent objective and subjective impacts on the transaction.

Consider, for example, a computer manufacturing company planning to acquire another business. The business to be acquired (the target) is a computer repair operation, and, once acquired, will be operated in support of its new parent. The buyer needs to borrow the greater part of the purchase price from a bank and wants to pledge the stock of the newly acquired subsidiary as collateral for the bank loan.

There are two kinds of values involved here. One is the price in the purchase transaction. The other is the security value the business will have as collateral. For the buyer, these two perspectives are opposing. The buyer naturally wants a lower price. The flip side is proof to a lender of a higher collateral value, which is desirable in order to obtain a larger loan or one with more favorable terms. If the collateral value is too low, the transaction may fail because the buyer will not be able to borrow enough money to consummate the purchase. But if the value expressed as purchase price is too high, the deal may fail for inadequate funds or, worse, go through and turn out to be an economic loser.

The seller's interest in the buyer's bank negotiations lies in seeing the transaction financed. Yet the seller also experiences some opposing tensions in wanting to characterize the transaction in the most favorable light for tax purposes, meaning a minimization of realized price and gain.

But to see the future...to seize the future...to maximize the future requires a close look not only at the present but, paradoxically, at the past. As the legend over the entrance to the National Archives in Washington, D.C., quoting Shakespeare, says, "What's Past is Prologue."

The classic definition of a market-determined price is a price arrived at between a fully informed, willing, and able buyer and a fully informed, willing, and able seller, neither being under any compulsion to transact. Yet in the real world one or both may be somehow compelled, and there is no such thing as a "fully informed" buyer or seller. Thus the collection, collation, management, analysis, and summary of data have a fundamental effect on the determination and realization of value, just as the selection of the materials an artist will sculpt has a dramatic impact on the appearance and worth of the final sculpture.

Selecting and obtaining information from the past and in the present is only half the job. The other half is the scrutiny of the information to be sure it has been obtained from the right sources, in the right quantities, and with the right qualities.

The first chapter deals with the initial steps of obtainment and scrutiny. All of that work in Chapter 1 is labeled Data Development.

Then the raw data must be manipulated, pondered, and organized into usable shape. Chapter 2, Analytical Framework, gets the materials ready for the price sculptor to begin carving.

By Chapter 3 the rough outlines of price begin to emerge. This contoured silhouette will be the output of a formula approach; a purely clinical approach to the pricing decision. It will not consider the distinctive character or peculiar nuances of the business, but will merely provide a precursor of the final price.

A sculptor may use several different techniques to first hew a recognizable outline before proceeding to the distinguishing detail work and the final polishing. Similarly, the clinical examination offers a choice of several numbers-crunching techniques. They are applicable no matter what kind of transaction is under consideration or what value is sought. These techniques will be reviewed in detail in Chapter 3, Financial Framework.

The best characteristic the techniques share is they provide a solid launching pad for value determination. Their dangerous characteristic is they may lull the analyst into a false sense of certainty. If one fails to look behind and beyond the numbers, the odds are very great that opportunities will be missed and hazards will be embraced in blind acceptance of what the computer spits out.

So, a similarly extensive description of the approach to subjective matters must also be undertaken if the detailing is going to polish to the right thicknesses in the right places. Businesses are vulnerable to so many different pressures, from personalities to economic factors to world events. As those pressures bear down, the business must be poised to seize the opportunities that sometimes result. Polishing under those conditions is no easy task.

Chapter 4, Value Components, examines the internal and external factors operating on the clinical price outline much as the sculptor might define the parts of the work to be polished and refined. It catalogues all the different sources of pressure and opportunity. It sets up a rational basis for sorting and selecting them, showing how even subjective tasks can be accomplished in an objective fashion.

Finally, those details will receive the appropriate refinement and polish to coalesce into a reliable pricing decision. Such decision making may be rigorous, but it need not be exhausting. Chapter 5, Components Assessment to Final Price, will explain how to make the rigors of decision making a purely productive effort, without fearful hairpulling or wasteful hairsplitting.

The merits of a work of art may be debated for generations. The merits of a price, however, can be tested in the marketplace. The business transactor does not have the luxury of leisurely reflection available to artists, for the hardscrabble world of the marketplace tolerates little delay. Events and time are all too ready to rough up the edges and smudge the precision of even the most thorough and elegant appraisal.

To find a price capable of withstanding those stresses in the course of producing an optimal transaction requires accurate and adequate data, carefully distilled and molded. It also requires a well organized approach to the detail without losing sight of the whole picture. The proper analytical tools must be selected. The analyst needs an appreciation of the environment and circumstances in which all these ingredients are blended. At last they are combined, and the catalyst of rigorous business judgment is brought to bear by the discipline of the process, producing a price decision in which the transactor can indeed have maximum confidence.

Chapter 1

Data Development

First Steps to Realistic Determination

BEHOLDER'S VIEW

A price a buyer cannot afford kills the transaction, whether it is too high by 1 percent or 100 percent. Affordability is just one of the factors considered in a price decision. The more a buyer desires a business, the greater the price the buyer is willing to pay.

In that sense the value one perceives is like beauty: It is in the eye of the beholder. To appreciate beauty, one must first see it. One can read about a great painting, talk about it, imagine it, but until one sees it, the greatness cannot truly be appreciated.

If there is a blemish, or a series of them, the painting will be considered less masterful, and, accordingly, will have less worth. On the other hand, a painting that is discovered to contain more than first meets the eye is of the greatest distinction.

A transactor who doesn't consider all of the value factors, including those that might not first meet the eye, is missing opportunities. And, one who overlooks the blemishes is likely to get into serious trouble. This statement is just as true for a seller as a buyer, because a seller who does not view his own business realistically risks selling too cheaply by pricing too low, or risks never converting his business into liquid assets by pricing too high.

To behold with 20/20 vision requires a complete examination of the subject matter.

TWO DATA SEGMENTS

The subject matter to be considered in valuing a business can be generally classified into two broad information categories:

1. *Subjective:*   Data that is qualitative in nature and not readily expressed by some quantifiable standard. Examples are the expertise of employees, the eye appeal of packaging, the company's sensitivity to political events, the health of a key employee, the reliability of suppliers, the militancy of labor unions.

2. *Objective:*   Data that is measurable by some kind of quantifiable standard. Examples are profits, units of sales, gross margin, debt coverage, turnover, GNP correlation, number of employees, advertising response.

Both kinds of data are prone to subjective interpretation. Both may be manipulated in objective ways. Each kind of data will often contain elements that might well be tagged as the other kind.

We need not concern ourselves at this point with precisely categorizing data that is sought or received. The conclusions—and further questions—drawn from the data are what count. Yet, having the two categories makes it easier to plan the procedure for analysis; and such planning is, as will be further explained, a crucial element in the chances for success of any valuation and pricing effort.

Nowhere is the distinction more useful than in obtaining input to the decision making, that is, in the development of the data itself. Like two different segments of the same market, the two types of data demand separate treatments if the analyst is going to get the most out of them.

Further, such treatments also must consider the separate but related problems that beset each. Then, when they're put together one can see the whole picture and make a reasonable, and hopefully optimal, pricing decision.

FIRST IMPRESSIONS

On the subjective side, the constant source of tension for the business analyst lies in the concern over when *some* information equals *enough* information. It is impossible to get perfect information, especially when dealing with a dynamic business in an ever changing economy influenced by swirling political, social, geophysical, and myriad other events. All those factors are more or less randomly perceived and processed by people, each with a unique psychological, intellectual, and emotional makeup.

Accordingly, any business can be studied endlessly, with the student safely (but foolishly) able to maintain that it's too soon to certify a value or a price, or even express an opinion on one, because enough information has not been acquired. On the other hand, it is at least equally imprudent to go off half-cocked with half-baked notions. Strangely enough, the more information available, and the more means of communication and inquiry at one's disposal, the greater the chance for a short circuit in the decision-making process caused by information overload.

Overload usually manifests itself in two ways. In one scenario, so much data is coming in that it cannot be organized into a meaningful picture. To avoid that scenario, the information is processed too rapidly, yielding scenario number two, which is an analysis filled with errors producing an incoherent picture.

The trick is to find the balance. At some point enough information, sufficiently well organized, will be on hand to give the transactor confidence to say "Go!" or "No go."

Objective methods, like ranking or weighting, can be applied to subjective data. For those tasks, or even for just keeping track of such information, ever more capable computers are a godsend. Nonetheless, the old adage "Garbage in, garbage out" still applies, so computers are no panacea. In fact, they are cursed with the fiendish twist that the more input, the greater the chance for error in output.

Often, data development is undertaken automatically, without real thought to the assumptions implied. Since output decisions depend on input data, it makes sense to spend some time formulating and testing the underlying assumptions. They will determine input and indirectly determine the decisive output.

For example, the core objective material for most business analysts will be a set of financial statements. The figures in the statements are usually accepted as the coordinates for determining where the business places on the fundamental initial pass/fail plot:

Is the business profitable?

Does it have a positive net worth?

Are sales growing?

How much debt does the company carry?

Industry by industry, there will be a few more first hurdle questions, but the point here is that first impressions matter a great deal, and accepting the financial statements *without a plan of review* is a risky proposition. Take the benchmark questions about profits, net worth, sales and debt:

Is the business profitable? The inventory method (LIFO, FIFO, etc.) employed by the company may make all the difference in showing a profit or loss on the statements.

Does it have a positive net worth? Similarly, the depreciation methods employed may seriously understate (or possibly overstate) the real net worth of the company.

Are sales growing? Depending on whether the Cash Accounting Method or the Accrual Accounting Method is used, the actual direction of sales may be misstated.

How much debt does the company carry? Off-balance sheet financing can radically understate the true level of a company's overall indebtedness.

No doubt most pros are going to consider these elementary accounting matters, but what will be the impact on the potential transactor who is far more involved in running a business than in valuing one? Moreover, even where a pro is calling the shots, without a systematic preface of assumption testing the analysis will be hit-or-miss depending upon what the pro remembers, what the pro stresses, and what issues surface in the unstructured—and potentially meandering—course of inquiry.

SOURCE ATTRIBUTES

Subjective question number one is "Where do we look for information?" The answer begs a second question, "What attributes should the sources of information have?"

The best sources will have all these attributes:

1. Provide accurate data. In other words, the information does not contain errors.

Test Question to ask: "Can the information be verified?"

2. Provide complete data. Not necessarily exhaustive, and not the one-stop place for all the data, but rather, for the issue under consideration, the data doesn't omit anything critical, meaning information that would materially change the output or the opinion of the evaluator. For example, take a company showing a big drop in insurance costs. Critical information would be the extent of change in insurance coverage, policy terms, and face values, to be sure the expenses are comparable in the different periods.

Test Question to ask: "What might be missing?"

3. Provide timely data. Out-of-date information isn't very useful.

Test Question to ask: "Given the age of the information, could significant change have occurred?"

4. Provide reliable data.   The information should not be skewed or misstated for some ulterior motive or on account of a bias. It should be truthful. The less trustworthy the source, the less credibility its information will have. For example, the data provided by a public relations firm for a company is sure to aim for the best image, while seeking to cover up blemishes.

Test Question to ask: "Does the source have an axe to grind?"

5. Easy to understand.   Data that is too complex is not preferred, because unraveling it adds costs and provides opportunity for error. Complex information should not be ignored merely because it is complex. Instead, if possible, it should be simplified by breaking it down, restating it, or summarizing it.

Test Question to ask: "Does the information make sense?"

6. Inexpensive to obtain.   As in any transaction, costs matter. The larger the transaction, the more one should be willing to spend to be sure it's properly evaluated. The more important the issue to the success of the transaction, the more it's worth to obtain the data.

Test Question to ask: "What's it going to cost?"

7. Easy to analyze.   The more well organized the data, the faster and cheaper the analysis can be accomplished, and the sooner a decision can be reached and implemented.

Test Question to ask: "How is the information presented?"

The company itself is often the first and the best source of information, but it is by no means the only one. Following is a checklist of additional sources to consider:

Bankers	Credit reporting agencies
Vendors	Trade associations
Unions	Regulators
Former employees	Public records
Customers	Public agencies
Former customers	Competitors

These outside sources can be useful to the seller, as well as the buyer. What outside advisors think of the seller's company should play a role in the seller's own determination, as the reactions of advisors are likely to be indicative of the reactions of a buyer. Experts may also be able to predict how a buyer's experts will advise a buyer.

WHAT INFORMATION?

The specifics of the question "What information?" will be considered in depth in Chapters 3 and 4. At this juncture, it is worth discussing the general guidelines for selecting information. Some information should be aggressively pursued. Some will be accepted if available. Some ought to be ignored or even discarded in order to prevent overload and being sidetracked by immaterial or irrelevant items.

The driving consideration in information selection is the nature of the business. The secondary consideration is the objective of the analysis. For example, a labor intensive business will demand more information about personnel, labor regulations affecting the industry, labor availability, payroll procedures and their effect on cash flow, productivity, and unionization. From another angle, a business in a mature industry will place greater stress on productivity and market share, while a business in a new, high-tech industry will place more emphasis on research and development capabilities.

As for the nature of the transaction, a buyer who will be borrowing from a bank to finance the transaction will need more solid data on collateral value of assets. Merger partners will want greater information on management procedures and compatibility of operating systems.

The central point is that information should not be collected willy-nilly. Plan the extent of information needed, and that means planning where, when, and how that information should be collected. Create a timetable and a customized, organized checklist. Then adhere to them.

Timetables are an especially important part of planning. Deciding when events should occur and how actions should be ordered is a branch of data development.

As data grows older and the market changes, prices become more tenuous; so the timetable cannot be too long. A buyer must set a time limit on investigation to avoid letting a good deal slip away and to prevent a bad deal from eating up the buyer's resources. A sales transaction usually stresses a business. Pricing and transacting divert effort from normal business operations, which both sides want to see successfully maintained. The parties must jointly control the timing of a deal to keep it on track and to prevent it from harming those operations.

SUBJECTIVE DATA DISTILLATION

Once data begins to flow, the analysis of its importance must be undertaken *before* one can start drawing conclusions from it. Data must be put into a form that makes it easy to analyze and that eliminates inherent inaccuracies, ambiguities, and misstatements.

When dealing with subjective data, the biggest problem is clarifying imprecise characterization.

For example, to say the plant is old is to invite the Henny Youngman retort, "Compared to what?" Such a characterization is easily remedied by reference to the objective standard, "The plant is 27 years old."

The danger is greater and the remedy less handy with a piece of data that says, for instance, "The labor situation is unstable, according to the Company's personnel director."

Certainly, he's in a position to know, but again, "Compared to what?" The Company's prior history? The rest of the industry? The record of the potential buyer? The local economy? The nation at large?

The question must be pursued and considered in the decision. The price is certain to be affected by it. The seller must consider defusing the problem.

But to be sure of its meaning, the statement must also be distilled. It must be put into language that makes sense and can be evaluated in terms of the Company's value and the upcoming transaction. All such statements should go through an Information Filter, to evaluate their potential impact and to distill them to a focused meaning, if the potential impact is significant.

Such a Filter should have the sequence shown in Figure 1.1. Let's run through the example. The "Subjective Data Received" is the following statement:

> The labor situation is unstable.

Test 1: "Is it *trustworthy?*"

What is the source of the information? Is it someone who has a reputation for honesty? If it comes from a publication, who's the author? Ultimately the question is "Does the maker of the statement have an axe to grind?" The greater the bias behind the statement, the less trustworthy it is.

Assume this statement was made by the personnel director, who has a reputation for honesty. The statement was made at the last annual meeting of shareholders, where there is a legal duty to be forthright. It was unchallenged by other company officials. So it appears trustworthy. By

Figure 1.1: Information Filter

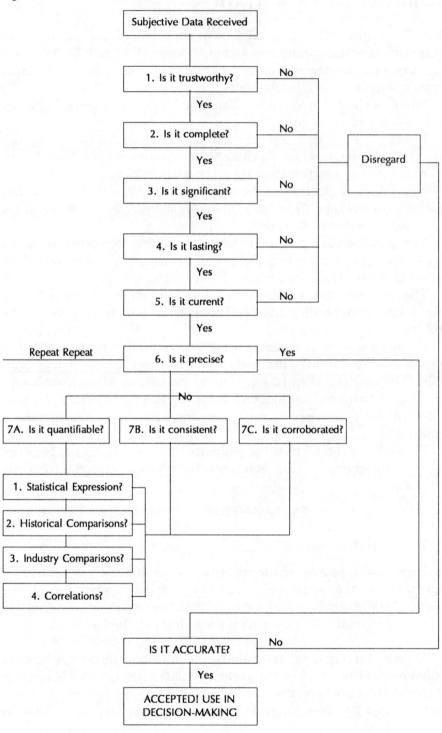

trustworthy we do not mean it is accepted as true but that the person making the statement believed it to be true.

Test 2: "Is it *complete?*"

If a statement is taken out of context or if the underlying concept is half-baked, it is not worth spending much time on it until the whole story is available. In this example, we'll presume the remainder of the personnel director's report was an elaboration on the basic theme and was obviously meant to be applied to the whole company, not just to one location or one group of employees.

Test 3: "Is it *significant?*"

Insignificant items do not deserve detailed analysis. Accountants would probably say "*Material* items deserve analysis." Materiality is a relative term, which varies with transaction size and according to the objectives of the analyst.

A company-wide labor problem would be significant, even if it doesn't lead to a strike. If the problem is already affecting production, it may have several ramifications. The bad news is if it is not corrected, margins and profits will be squeezed, validating a lower price. The good news is it may indicate greater productive capacity yet to be tapped. If so, the business justifies a higher price.

Test 4: "Is it *lasting?*"

A transitory problem, which is not likely to show up again or which is not going have any major impact on the company, is not worth detailed examination. Labor unrest is too critical a problem to ignore. It is one of those kinds of difficulties that may be symptomatic of deeper problems, such as management incompetence. It can easily resurface. It is virtually certain to demand resources to solve and will sap resources if left unsolved. Treat it as lasting.

Test 5: "Is it *current?*"

Information may be outdated, but not apparently so. The age of information is always important. The weightier the statement, the older it can be and still be considered current. For example, a statement made six months ago that salesmen are exceeding their entertainment budgets is probably obsolete. But a statement also made six months ago that the company seems to be losing its technological edge in product development (especially if product development and life cycles are lengthy) is considered recent and deserves attention.

A statement about labor relations made at an annual meeting just a few months ago is still recent enough to demand further investigation, given the gravity of the matter.

Test 6: "Is it *precise?*"

Virtually any sort of subjective statement, especially one that characterizes with adjectives, needs clarification, if not verification. The intensity or extent of a problem is almost as important as the mere existence of the problem.

As we've already seen, this particular statement about labor is not precise. Now, how to make it precise? On to the next level, the distillation tests.

THE DISTILLATION TESTS

One way to define the statement's outline more clearly is by quantifying as much as possible some of its aspects, leading us to:

Test 7A: "Is it *quantifiable?*"

Quantification may be accomplished using the subtests. It is a way of breaking down the problem into smaller elements thereby bringing the whole into sharper focus. If we say we've seen a big animal, the statement may be true, but it lacks precision. If we say the animal stood about seven feet high on four legs, weighed about a half ton, had one trunk and two tusks, it sounds like we saw an elephant.

7A-1: Statistical Expression

Some of the statistics that might be developed on labor unrest would include:

Grievances filed

Productivity levels

Quality control statistics

Absenteeism

Labor turnover rates (quit and hire; separation; instability, etc.)

Inventory shrinkage (indicating theft and vandalism)

Dependency program statistics (alcohol/drug use may be indicative)

Safety statistics (indicating inattention or disinterest)

7A-2: Historical Comparisons

Once statistics are developed, how do they measure up against prior history? Are they higher or lower than a month ago? A year ago? The last time there was a strike or other labor difficulty?

7A-3: Industry Comparisons

How do the statistics compare with those of other companies in the industry? If our labor statistics are not remarkably dissimilar, they tend to contradict the statement, unless the whole industry is having trouble.

One note of caution here: Be sure the calculations are made on a comparable basis. For example, a company with 10,000 employees is almost certainly going to have a higher number of labor grievances filed than a company with 500. The number should be tested on some comparable basis, such as grievances per 100 employees or per 1000 manhours.

7A-4: Correlations

Statistical methods of correlation (for example, least squares, curve fitting, beta coefficients, etc.) can be employed to further test for statistical accuracy and meaning. Correlative methods are also good for making base forecasts, which we will be exploring in a later chapter.

Test 7B: "Is it *consistent?*"

The second means of evaluating imprecise data is to test for consistency. In other words, has the company experienced these kinds of problems before? Frequently? Recently? What happened in the past? Did it appear the difficulties were really solved or were the symptoms just covered up, merely postponing the day of reckoning?

Test 7C: "Is is *corroborated?*"

Are there other pieces of data that tend to confirm or deny the statement? For example, if labor leaders are professing positive feelings toward the company and the union's newsletter is similarly upbeat, the statement would seem to be inconsistent. It is also important to consider the reliability of the corroborating or contradictory statements.

When all is said and done, the ultimate question presents itself:

IS IT ACCURATE?

If yes, it qualifies for inclusion in the pricing process. However, if it is accepted, but doubts are still harbored, the analyst should retain a healthy skepticism in the event that later information or events prove it does not deserve inclusion.

OBJECTIVE DATA DISTILLATION

The principal pieces of objective information are the financial statements. Management reports, tax returns, regulatory filings, legal documents, and third-party information (from Dun & Bradstreet, for example) are the major backups.

Despite Generally Accepted Accounting Principles (GAAP), there are still great possibilities for substantial differences in stating the financial condition and performance of the same entity. Moreover, many smaller companies and many of the internal reporting figures used by larger companies do not conform to GAAP. And, perhaps most critically, many decision makers are not fluent in GAAP in the first place.

Therefore, financial information must be massaged and might even be rewritten to conform to the accounting concepts of the analyst, if it is to yield the hard data on which sound decisions can be based. One of the big hurdles for many analysts is the failure to recognize that there are really at least seven ways to consider the accounting for a particular company:

1. Book Accounting
2. Cash Flow Accounting
3. Budgetary Accounting
4. Management Accounting
5. Tax Accounting
6. Operational Accounting
7. Regulatory Accounting

Book Accounting

Book Accounting encompasses the activities attendant to the production of financial statements. Because of the standards imposed by GAAP and the conventions necessary for developing financial statements (for example, the somewhat arbitrary assignment of lives to assets for the purpose of charging periodic depreciation), Book Accounting can distort what is actually happening. It also is not particularly susceptible to certain types of vital financial analysis, because the limited number of accounts frequently mixes transactions more easily analyzed if separated. These shortcomings are often exaggerated in highly regulated industries, such as public utilities, whose charts of accounts are prescribed in detail by regulation.

Yet, every company must have its set of books, whether in a 5" x 7" notebook or on a hard disk. Financial statements are a logical starting point and their premises are the norm of evaluation. The essential normative figures of Book Net Worth, Total Liabilities, Net Assets, Book Profit, and Interest Coverage all have very real meaning in the quest for a fair price.

Cash Flow Accounting

Cash Flow Accounting details the actual movement of funds. As a required part of today's certified financial statements, Cash Flow Accounting is usually the number two system behind Book Accounting. It has special worth in determining the true viability of the entity, for a company with all the profits in the world but without adequate cash to support operations will find itself insolvent. Cash Flow Accounting is also critical for prognosticating the amount of resources a buyer will need to infuse (or be able to draw out) if a transaction is consummated. That is critical information for measuring the buyer's rate of return.

Budgetary Accounting

Budgetary Accounting consists of two equally important phases. The first is the future-oriented planning and establishment of goals and spending targets designed to achieve those goals at least cost. The second phase is the measurement of results against those goals and targets.

Budgetary Accounting is the insider's view of a company's performance and of its goals, which relate, or should relate, very closely to the company's view of its own capabilities and capacities. This information, if it can be obtained by outsiders, has tremendous value.

Management Accounting

Management Accounting concentrates on analysis of corporate activities for management decision making. The function of Management Accounting is to provide cogent data on which decisions can be based, often involving input of assumptions and matching of information not otherwise connected within the traditional accounting framework.

Much of Management Accounting concerns itself with forecasting and contingency planning. Obviously, this kind of information will be very useful in a pricing decision, not only for fixing the price but also for indicating risk levels.

Management Accounting information should be readily available to the insider, but may be tough to obtain for the outsider. Note, too, that even when obtained it may be difficult for an outsider to interpret; because managers will often employ their own shortcuts, which may not be understood by an outsider.

Tax Accounting

Tax Accounting focuses, of course, on the determination of the minimum legitimate tax liability, the development of the documentation to defend and support the determination, and the timely preparation and filing of tax returns.

Tax returns and their supporting documentation are very important in sales of closely held businesses. As they may be the only statements assembled with the help of a professional accountant, and as the spectre of prosecution for tax fraud promotes (but doesn't guarantee) honest accounting, the tax returns may well be the most accurate financial statements available, even though they may be skewed by the peculiarities of regulation.

Buyers should compare them to other financial statements provided by a seller, even if others are accountant-prepared. Conversely, for a seller preparing his own statements, the tax returns give useful parameters for preparation; and the seller should be prepared to explain to the buyer the reasons for variation between tax returns and other statements. For all businesses, analysis of the tax returns is still a necessary step to:

1. Insure there are no latent tax liabilities that may arise in the future, either because of legal deferral or illicit treatments.

2. To determine if there are unused tax attributes, such as loss carryforwards or credits, which may add to the value, especially for a buyer able to use them to shelter profits. Naturally, the buyer must check to be sure the tax benefits are transferable to the buyer, as some kinds can be extinguished by a sale.

3. To determine if changes might be made in the Tax Accounting procedures to limit the tax bite and improve the after-tax profits or cash flow or both. It is worth noting that a change in ownership frequently provides the best opportunity to obtain approval from tax authorities for such changes, if approval is mandatory.

Don't, by the way, ignore state and local tax returns, as they may also provide insight and opportunities. For example, a buyer may be able to move operations from a high-tax jurisdiction to a lower taxed one, thereby creating savings and wringing more value from a transaction. Local taxes tend to concentrate more on assets, as opposed to income taxes, which focus on profits. Local tax data is therefore more important in an asset-intensive business, but also is a useful way to help verify the supposed worth and characteristics of taxed assets.

Operational Accounting

Operational Accounting is the statistical and nonfinancial recordkeeping absolutely essential for relating pure dollars to operations. It includes matters like productivity statistics, human resources, and industrial management data. With these materials, the analyst has the very best chance to relate the accountant's cold data to the real world of goods delivered, services performed, overhead needs fulfilled, and the "blood, toil, tears and sweat" of the factory floor or the order desk.

These nonfinancial figures are often the most overlooked and the least understood by accounting and financial types. It is just as hard for an accountant to viscerally grasp the meaning of an engineer's plot of metal stress at varying machine speeds as it is for the engineer to viscerally grasp adjusting entries to match book inventory to physical count. No doubt each can intellectually understand the procedures of the other, but the full implications of the numbers are likely to escape each outside his or her own field.

So, when operational data can be obtained by a buyer, it should be reviewed by an expert in the field. Even if the buyer possesses the expertise, a second opinion, reached without the stress of being in the transaction, will often prove valuable, particularly when it can be matched against the financial statements. On the other hand, the seller may want to focus the buyer on some of the operational data and be sure the buyer fully understands it, so a better case can be made for the seller's asking price.

Regulatory Accounting

Regulatory Accounting is simply recordkeeping in compliance with the requirements of any governmental unit. While often thought to be the concern of only a limited number of industries, one gets the impression that the regulatory trend seems to be to include at least some of the operations of more and more kinds of companies, on Federal, state, local, and even foreign levels.

Much like Tax Accounting, the output from Regulatory Accounting should be examined to see if there are additional opportunities or lurking dangers, which may later impact the values of the company.

To flesh out the accounting types, following are two schematics. The first (Figure 1.2) shows the treatments of the purchase of a $100,000 machine. Regulatory Accounting is left out of the first schematic because the effects are all going to be determined by the nature of the regulation, which are not necessarily pegged to any well recognized standard.

The second schematic (Figure 1.3) summarizes the attributes of each type of accounting, including Regulatory Accounting.

AVOIDING DATA BIAS

Do a good enough job in collecting data, and it's not difficult to suffer "information overload." Care must be taken to be sure the most useful information is given the highest priority. Human nature being what it is, appropriate priorities are not easy to assign.

Consider the following axioms that generally hold true as to the influence particular pieces of data are likely to have:

Data more recently received will tend to have greater influence than data previously received.

Figures tend to have greater influence than narratives.

Charts, graphs, and other "pictorials" tend to have greater influence than raw figures or narratives.

Information in a simpler form will have greater influence than information which is more complex.

Information received from someone well liked by the recipient will have greater influence than information received from someone less well liked or from someone disliked.

Information neatly and appealingly presented will have greater influence than information sloppily presented.

Surprising information tends to have greater influence than unsurprising information.

Some people are biased toward oral data, others toward written data. Know which bias you have, to control its effects.

The point of all these axioms, of course, is having greater influence

Figure 1.2: Transaction Accounting Analysis

	BOOK	CASH FLOW	BUDGET	MANAGEMENT	TAX	OPERATIONS
Calculations for this Year	Rev $1,000,000 Exp −900,000 Pretax $ 100,000 Machine purchase is capitalized.	In $1,000,000 Out: Exp −900,000 Mach −100,000 Net In 0	Has this machine purchase been contemplated in capital budget?	What impact on year-end ratios, credit rating, and market acceptance?	Depreciation reduces tax by $10,000, increasing net.	No impact on present year.
Impact on Future Years	Increase pretax expenses by depreciation. Choose depreciation method.	Add back depreciation to eliminate effect of non-cash expense.	Increases in maintenance and carrying charges for responsible unit.	Calculate expected annual incremental profit from use and determine return on investment.	Depreciation reduces annual tax liability. Local personal property tax increased.	Determine productivity increases expected, including learning curve. What impact on break-even? Should prices be adjusted?
Reconciliation to Book	NA	Capital expenditure is not expensed, creating this year's difference. Future years differ by depreciation.	Depreciation is "noncontrollable" expense and therefore not in area budgets.	Show impact on selected accounts.	Show impact on tax accounts.	Show impact on selected revenue and expense accounts.
Conclusions	No effect on this year's pretax profits. Depreciation in future years will reduce profits unless offset by gains due to operation. Control expenses carefully during test period.	Cash shortage may result while awaiting payback. Short-term borrowings may require consideration; possibly lease or finance machine.	Purchase may generate cost pressures in maintenance budget. Can temporary cutbacks be made in other areas until machine is proven?	Machine will yield sufficient ROI if operated properly. Monitor downtime closely and be sure sales are absorbing production.	Tax consequences mitigate real cost.	Productivity management crucial to project success. Be sure sales is kept aware of cost profile to determine pricing and discount strategies.

Figure 1.3: Summary of Accounting Types

ACCOUNTING TYPE	GOALS	REPORTS	EXAMPLES OF OUTPUT	PITFALLS
BOOK	Determine profitability and net worth of entity.	Financial statements.	Profits, net worth.	Constrained by GAAP, etc. Can lack specificity. Strictly historic data.
CASH FLOW	Understand changes in cash positions, determine cash needs, and match availability.	Cash flow statement; cash forecast; cash reconciliation.	Cash balances; cash needs; cash available.	Fails to elucidate commitments, obligations, and noncash transactions.
BUDGETARY	Control expenditures. Set targets and provide performance motivation and measurement.	Budgets; variances.	Targets; performance.	Lines of authority do not necessarily follow functional logic.
MANAGEMENT	Analyze activities to plan and improve.	Special purpose reports.	Investment decisions, etc.	Relation to book and other reports can be distorted.
TAX	Compliance and liability minimization.	Tax returns.	Tax payments and refunds.	Artificial requirements not useful for nontax decisions.
OPERATIONAL	Control and planning of nonfinancial aspects of activities.	Special purpose reports.	Units of output, employment, etc.	Not always subject to accurate quantification.
REGULATORY	Compliance and best case to receive regulatory approval.	Special purpose reports; required filing.	Rate base; compliance reports.	Artificial requirements distort and not useful for nonregulatory decisions.

doesn't mean the information *deserves* greater influence. Even its deserving greater influence won't mean it will be properly interpreted or accurately applied. A relatively constant effort at monitoring and straining out biases is a real plus in the process. This is most easily accomplished by subjecting the analyst and the analysis to questioning from additional people, especially trustworthy, talented, and knowledgeable outsiders with no vested interest in the transaction other than seeing the truth. The need for secrecy often mitigates against just such scrutiny, so attaining the right balance is a triumph of effective transaction management.

DATA ORGANIZATION

With bias under control, our mission is to organize the data to answer a series of questions about the entity. The questions will vary with the nature of the transaction and the parties considering it. The types of questions to be answered will be addressed in later chapters. To make the best preparations, the data should be prioritized by importance and categorized by area of concern as part of the organization process. Once again, the distinction between objective and subjective data is useful when considering organization of data.

At this stage, handling the objective data is relatively easy. For the most part it can be loaded into a data base computer program to give a ready statistical picture of the company. To illustrate that, we introduce Sample Company in Appendix 1 with a financial and statistical history, although it is somewhat brief to simplify our examples.

Organization of subjective data occupies more time. For the subjective data, compilation of a few lists that prioritize the subjective data, or mingling it with objective data, is the principal data organization effort.

One list should outline in order, from most important to least important, the advantages and disadvantages of the transaction. For example, a buyer considering purchasing a smaller competitor could develop this list:

Transaction Advantages

Improves customer service	Improves company image
Provides sales leads → increases sales	Better technical abilities
Rate of return above cost of capital	Better research capacity
Expands product lines	More management depth
Increases operating leverage	Some geographical expansion
Increases earnings stability	

Transaction Disadvantages	
Heavy debt load	Greater lender restrictions
Fractioantes management efforts	Some undesirable locations
Involves unionized workers	Higher insurance costs

Some of these items may have their own sublists that elaborate on the issue. All items should be traceable to backup documentation, explaining the reasons for each conclusion.

As you can see, too, there is not necessarily a match between related items. For example, "Some geographical expansion" is the least important advantage, while the related "Some undesirable locations" is not the last disadvantage. But when focusing on a particular issue, the list will be restructured to match points and counterpoints.

Another way to use the list is to take each item and give it a weight based on intuitive factors to produce a "Net Advantages Score." Taking the just completed list, assume each of the items could be ranked from 1 to 10 as to importance, 10 being the most important. Then the following might result:

Transaction Advantages	Rank	Transaction Disadvantages	Rank
Improves customer service	9	Heavy debt load	10
Provides leads → increase sales	7	Fractionates management efforts	5
ROR above cost of capital	7	Involves unionized workers	4
Expands product lines	4	Greater lender restrictions	3
Increases operating leverage	3	Some undesirable locations	3
Increases earnings stability	3	Higher insurance costs	2
Improves company image	2		
Better technical abilities	1		
Better research capacity	1		
More management depth	1		
Some geographical expansion	1		
TOTALS	39		27

NET ADVANTAGES SCORE: 39 − 27 = +12

Grafting an objective method like this onto a subjective set of information has appeal. First check your biases in doing so, to be sure the rankings aren't unrealistic and the score derived doesn't become some kind of shallow decision-making surrogate. This type of manipulation should be just one more arrow in the quiver designed to lead to a clear determination of price.

Furthermore, this kind of ranking can also help to pinpoint difficulties with a transaction, which might lead to better focus for improving the structure of a deal. For example, the highest ranking disadvantage—in fact the highest ranking item—is "Heavy debt load." Maybe the transaction will be more appealing, and the seller's price can be profitably met, if some equity flavor could be added to finance part or all of the transaction. More common stock? Preferred stock? Convertible debt?

An exercise like this is useful even for deals that don't go through to see where the problems were and to help shape perspectives for the next time around. Although we've used a buyer's list here, a seller's list has equal value for the seller, to see where the fly (or flies) were in the ointment. It may lead to figuring out how a future sale should be pitched or how the company should be changed in some way to make the best price more easily achievable.

Then there is the "Opportunities and Risks" list. Opportunities are the things that aren't counted on but can go right to make the deal a bigger winner. Risks are the things that can go wrong to make it a loser.

Again the subjectivity might be "objectified" to some degree by assigning both probabilities *and* rankings to each of the contingencies, multiplying them to get a probabilistic impact ranking and again deriving a net score. The same caveats about bias apply, as well as caveats about potential errors in judgment. Following is an example:

Opportunities/Risks	Likely %	Rank	Probable Rank
Opportunities:			
Upgraded product line with jump on competition from more serviceable products producing more sales	75	8	6.00
Better engineering cuts manufacturing costs	70	5	3.50
Greater market penetration from more service contacts	60	4	2.40
Liquidation of some subsidiary assets produces significant cash	90	2	1.80
TOTAL OPPORTUNITIES SCORES		19	13.70

Opportunities/Risks	Likely %	Rank	Probable Rank
Risks:			
Integration of operations cannot be successfully accomplished	20	10	2.00
Combined operation produces greater overhead	30	7	2.10
Repair operations require greater cash support for higher levels of spare parts inventories and larger geographic area coverage	50	3	1.50
Personnel not meshing creates internal conflicts	25	2	0.50
TOTAL RISKS SCORES		22	6.10

Net Probabilistic Score: 13.70 – 6.10 = +7.60

Net Unweighted Score: 19 – 22 = –3

A few comments about these results:

1. Listing order is again by raw rank to indicate importance if the possibility reaches fruition. Some may prefer to list by probability, so the most likely event is shown first. Still others may desire to list from highest net probability to lowest.

2. The Net Probabilistic Score is the probabilistic outcome based on the analyst's view of the contingencies. The Net Unweighted Score is also important, telling what the outcome will be if all the events occur. In this case, the net result would be negative, which should not be surprising as the first-listed risk has a 10 ranking, and essentially indicates on its own that the takeover isn't going to fulfill its objectives.

3. It is always possible to add to a risk list, by conjuring up all sorts of gremlins and spooks that can make things go wrong. The really remote possibilities and those issues whose impact would be negligible should be left out to avoid skewing the list. However, if there is an inclination to add many minor points in one direction or the other, it may hint at an intuitive feeling—or a bias—and deserves some additional consideration.

4. Lastly, remember not to allow the tool to substitute artificially for good business judgment.

ONWARD

Data development is a lot of work and probably the most tedious part of the pricing process. Although it won't guarantee an optimum outcome, if done well, it will go a long way toward improving the odds.

The other parts of the pricing process, while less tedious, are no less demanding. Onward to the procedures for analysis of all this carefully collected, culled, and collated critical data.

Chapter 2

Analytical Framework
The Essential Decision Tools

FROM INDIFFERENCE TO INTENSITY

The transaction for the sale of a business is no different from any other commercial transaction: If it is to occur, it must independently appear to make sense to the buyer and seller. A transaction will look like it makes sense when it seems to present a better opportunity than not entering into the transaction.

The big question is whether either or both participants are correct in their perceptions. The principal standard for answering that question is the standard of Return on Investment, whether the investor is cashing in as seller or anteing up in anticipation of future returns as buyer. One of the nice things about the standard of a business transaction is that it can be measured objectively.

Perfect measurement (as in so much of life) can be obtained only in hindsight. What counts toward perception at the time of transaction is foresight. What this chapter reveals are the ways to develop transactional foresight, to see at least the basic outline of the future in the form of the objective standard of Return on Investment, which is the key to the right pricing decision.

ECONOMICS 101

It is useful to digress for a moment and borrow two concepts from Economics 101:

Indifference Points

Supply and Demand Curves

An Indifference Point is, for our purposes, a price at which a transactor would just as soon enter into the transaction as not do so. In other words the transactor is indifferent.

As the price goes up, the buyer gets closer and closer to his or her Indifference Point, the extreme maximum price the buyer is willing to pay. Conversely, as the price goes down, the seller gets closer and closer to his or her Indifference Point, the extreme minimum price the seller is willing to accept. These two mutually critical points can be graphically displayed on a line graph like that pictured in Figure 2.1.

The buyer is willing to buy anywhere from zero along the buyer's Line of Acceptability, up to the buyer's Indifference Point. Similarly, the seller is willing to transact anywhere from a theoretically infinite price down along the seller's Line of Acceptability to the minimum. Within the range the two lines share, the "Negotiation Zone," a sale can occur.

Once in a great while, the two Indifference Points will be precisely the same, which means the transaction will occur readily. More often than not, the two points will not reach each other, and no deal will be consummated.

Even if the two lines do reach, there's no guarantee the deal will be

Figure 2.1: Line Graph: Indifference Points

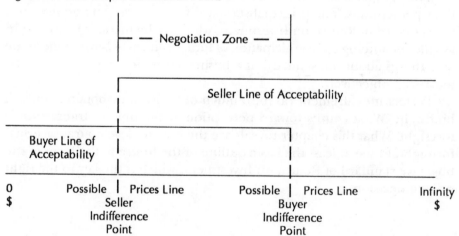

completed. There may be another buyer who makes the deal first. Other circumstances may intervene. Nonprice terms may prevent a deal from being made. But without a meeting of the lines on price, there can be no meeting of the minds on a transaction.

When the two lines do reach each other, though, just where within the Negotiation Zone will the deal price be marked? Figure 2.2, Typical Supply and Demand Curves, will provide an answer.

Adam Smith, in *The Wealth of Nations* first defined supply and demand curves, showing the price at which the market would settle (sometimes called the equilibrium price) given a particular supply and demand, like that pictured in Figure 2.2.

The theory is that as more supply, comes on the market, sellers will lower the price to sell the surplus. And, as more buyers enter the market or demand a greater quantity of product, the more they'll be willing to pay. If price drops due to excess supply, more buyers will want to buy. If price rises because of greater demand, more sellers will want to sell. At some point ("X" in Figure 2.2) there will be a matchup, meaning a transaction occurs.

But with a business sale there is only a single business under consideration. There is no range of quantity. So, instead of evaluating Price against Quantity, substitute Price against Intensity of Desire to depict the transaction. By Intensity of Desire, we mean the degree of willingness to enter into the transaction, which will be higher for the buyer as the price declines, but

Figure 2.2: Typical Supply and Demand Curves: Price versus Quantity

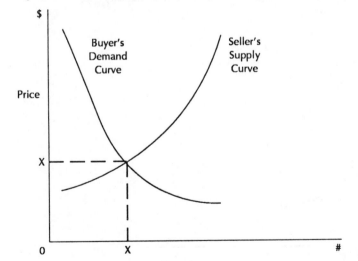

higher for the seller as the price rises. When there is a matchup of Intensities at a particular price point, the transaction occurs. That idea will produce a graphic with an intersecting price point like that pictured in Figure 2.3.

Note that the Price axis of the graph is a compressed, upright version of the Indifference Point Line Graph in Figure 2.1. By incorporating it into this supply/demand format, a theoretical determination of the price point of the transaction can indeed be portrayed.

While it is true the Intensity of Desire we've defined cannot be precisely quantified, all this picture-making yields a device for visualizing how the essential analytical tools may affect the outcome as those very tools are employed by buyers and sellers.

Specifically, moving the Indifference Point by defining a changed Range of Acceptability will affect the chances for accomplishing the deal. Or, changing the Intensity at one or more prices has the same impact of increasing or reducing the chances, depending on whether Intensity is heightened or lessened. All that is a function of the perception of the buyer and seller, each making independent decisions, but each influenced by the developed data and its manipulation.

So, having developed the data as detailed in Chapter 1, it's now time to manipulate it to get the baseline Indifference Points, an initial handle on Intensity along the Line of Acceptability, and, possibly, an idea of what the transaction counterpart is likely to be thinking.

Figure 2.3: Modified Supply and Demand Curves: Price versus Intensity

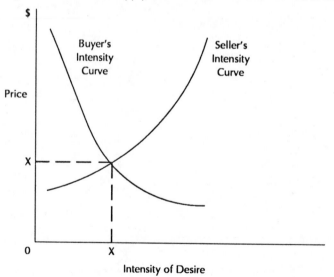

MORE ABOUT "SAMPLE COMPANY"

To illustrate the use of these various tools, we'll be using the concrete example of "Sample Company," a privately held business in the computer field made up of three parts:

Part 1 sells merchandise, specifically computers and accessories, most of which are purchased for resale, putting Sample in the distribution business.

Part 2 involves manufacturing. A relatively small portion of the accessories are manufactured by Sample. These items are low-tech accessories, such as plastic paper feeders, disk boxes, and the like.

Part 3 is the service end of the business, entailing installation and repair of computer systems.

So, Sample Company has characteristics of both a sales and a service operation. That is important, because the nature of the business can affect the applicability of some of the analytical tools or the proper interpretation of their output. For example, book value tends to be more meaningful in a sales operation as there are usually more tangible assets to correlate to business value than in a service outfit.

Appendix 1 contains 7-year summaries of financial and statistical information on Sample Company. Is seven years realistic? Is it too many years, too few? In the computer field, with its relatively rapid rate of technological change, using data that is too old may be misleading. On the other hand, having too little historical data may also be misleading.

Seven years covers both up and down business cycles. In fact, the financial information on Sample Company shows some down years in its own fortunes. We further discover that seven years covers more than one product life cycle and exceeds the average product lifespan, or period in which its customers keep its computer products. Going back fewer than five years is rarely advisable (except of course when the business isn't even that old) because it becomes statistically risky to be looking at so few pieces of data.

So, we're already making some necessarily subjective judgments, but we're doing so with conscious thought. And, just because we have seven years doesn't mean we will always use all seven. Nor does it mean we're foreclosed from going back and asking for more. (But, beware of getting too little data up front, as asking again and recalculating can mean delay that may be fatal to a deal.)

As we pace through the examples in this and other chapters, we may change the scenario or even some of the numbers they reflect about

Sample. Depending on the scenario, we could find very different motivations; that is, different shapes of the curve of Intensity of Desire, which will have a big effect on Indifference Point and the best price. We may not be able to trace those curves exactly, but we'll know 'em when we see 'em.

COMPONENTS OF RETURN

Before employing these tools to get a handle on value and price, let's look briefly at the components of return. Most investors talk about the term "profit" in an unspecific way, but profit has more than one possible meaning. To remove all doubt, these are the components of return we'll be interested in from the standpoint of the buyer or seller, as owner or potential owner:

Income: The sum of:

> Payouts (dividends from a corporation, distributions from a partnership, withdrawals from a sole proprietorship);
>
> Salary (or wages) for the owner; and
>
> Benefits (insurance, expense accounts, autos, etc.) for the owner.

Wealth Accumulation, which is the increase in the value of the ownership interest, realizable as the business (or a part of it) is resold. "Accumulation" may also be negative, if the value of the business declines.

Tax Effects, which may be positive (tax savings) or negative (additional taxes) and which may alter the Income received or Wealth Accumulation, or both.

One can also imagine some other intangible benefits that may be derived, such as the prestige of business ownership or the psychic rewards many find in managing a business. But for the moment at least, endeavoring as we are to develop a realistic baseline value, we'll stick to purely quantifiable economic rewards. It is also worth noting that the ability of the business to produce these benefits is dependent upon the business's internal financial performance, which will be reflected in three components:

> Profits, by which we mean the true amount by which revenues exceed costs (recalling the Chapter 1 discussion of accounting vagaries);
>
> Cash Flow; and
>
> Net Asset increase, as measured in terms of excess of market value (which is likely to be different from book value) over indebtedness.

The relationship between these two sets of components is obviously symbiotic. An unprofitable business cannot make payouts indefinitely, afford opulent salaries or abundant benefits, and will have a hard time increasing in value. Reciprocally, an owner who eviscerates the company by insisting on unreasonable payouts or salaries will be destroying, or at least hindering, the ability of the business to yield positive internal financials. Consequently, a part of the evaluation process will necessarily require a look at the relationship between the two sets of components in any given situation.

RISK AND RETURN

If rate of return on investment is the key to price, uncertainty about the rate creates uncertainty about the price. The price will also be a function of how prospectively certain (that is, risky) the achievement of a forecasted rate of return will be. These three factors—price, rate of return, risk—may be graphically conceptualized as in Figure 2.4.

As risk increases (certainty declines) the price at any single expected rate of return will be less, because there is an increasing chance the actual rate of return will not measure up to expectations.

Thus, though three separate businesses, perhaps in the same industry, are expected to yield x percent rate of return, they carry three substantially different prices.

Company "a" with the lowest risk is likely to be well established, with a

Figure 2.4: Risk Effect on Price: Constant Rate of Return

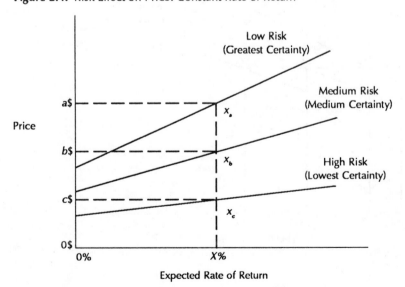

proven management, product line, and track record, thereby commanding the highest price of $a.

Company "b" has a somewhat more erratic track record, and tends to be more of a "me-too" factor, rather than a leader, in the industry (or locality). Perhaps it's struggling with some transient problem—a lawsuit, a scandal, labor unrest, and so forth—which casts doubt on the future fundamentals. Hence, the greater uncertainty means a value of only $b.

Meanwhile, Company "c" may be a startup, a perpetual also-ran, or a company with a poor quality-control reputation. It suffers from some disadvantage or combination of disadvantages, leaving its potential, or even its survival, a question of some gravity. So, its value is only $c.

These risk-defined differences will be reflected in P–E ratios, cap rates, and discount rates later on.

In a related vein, companies may have equal prices, but differing rates of return, resulting from disparities in risk, as depicted in Figure 2.5.

It is also worth noting that in all these examples, even at a 0.0 percent rate of return, the companies are not shown as having a zero-dollar value, regardless of risk, because the balance sheet and off-balance sheet assets (such as customer lists) acquired in a sale presumably will have residual or liquidation value. (Of course, it is theoretically possible to have both a negative expected rate of return and/or a negative net worth, in which creditor claims swamp the liquidation value for the owners. However, such

Figure 2.5: Risk Effect on Price: Varying Rates of Return

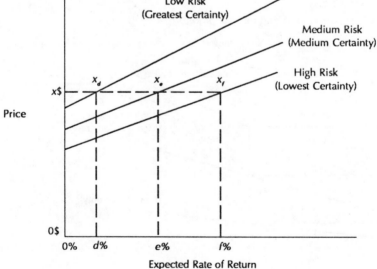

companies are destined to eventually—sooner rather than later—disappear.)

COST OF CAPITAL

Another critical point is that rate of return is necessarily a function of the buyer's cost of capital, as well as the target's revenue–expense profile. This axiom is often misperceived, especially by sellers, who tend to set a value by focusing on the profits and assets of their business, as if all buyers will have matching capital availability. The only circumstance in which that will be true is a deal with 100 percent seller financing on identical terms open to all buyers.

Cost of capital is usually envisioned as a blended or weighted cost as in the following example:

Capital Type	Capital	Annual Cost	Weight
Secured Debt	$1,000,000	8.0%	80,000
Unsecured Debt	500,000	10.0	50,000
Preferred Stock	100,000	12.0	12,000
Common Equity	400,000	15.0	60,000
Totals	$2,000,000		202,000
Weighted Average Cost		10.1%	

While this is a somewhat simplified schematic, it does illustrate some salient points.

1. Cost does tend to escalate as the security's claim on assets declines in priority.

2. This schematic has been simplified by ignoring tax consequences, so it could be refined to an after-tax cost.

3. Weight does not necessarily equal servicing costs paid out, as the weight should be calculated on an annualized basis. Changes occurring during the year probably will not match up.

4. An Average Cost of Capital is calculated at a specific point in time. Like any calculation derived from the financial statements, the degree to which it will be representative of the company's true average cost during the year will be a function of how stable the financial statements turn out to be. If a company cleans up debt at year end, or takes advantage of accounting devices, the statements can be deceiving.

5. Average Cost of Capital (sometimes called Embedded Cost of Capital) should not be confused with Marginal Cost of Capital, which is the amount the company will have to pay to attract the next dollar of capital. If that next dollar will be more debt, a new lender may well demand a higher rate because of the already high debt–equity ratio. It will certainly charge a market rate, regardless of past history.

Remember, we're talking about the buyer's cost of capital. If the buyer is a corporation, the cost of capital will look like the foregoing blended example as derived from the financials. If the buyer is an individual, cost of capital will be a blend of his interest rate(s) if he borrows, plus the assigned cost on his own capital put into the deal.

Realistic assigning of the cost of capital is not merely a function of stated interest rates (though they are usually the largest element) but also is a function of:

Opportunity Cost

The alternatives for investment should have an important impact on a buyer's views about deployment of capital. Arguably, even more than the definite alternatives, choices just over the horizon of which the buyer is only dimly aware may impel the buyer to hold more resources back. Thus, as more capital is committed now, the buyer's opportunity cost goes up if the accepted return is going to be lower than the future foregone return. The cost will be higher even though the future return may be unknown at the moment the buyer accepts the present return by committing the capital.

To illustrate, assume $100,000 carrying a stated cost of capital (interest rate on the borrowed funds) of 15 percent is committed to earn a 20 percent gross return. Weeks later another opportunity, which would yield 25 percent, is passed up, because the capital has been committed to the first deal. The opportunity cost is:

$$25\% - 20\% = 5\%.$$

Adding 5 percent to the 15 percent stated cost means a total cost of 20 percent for a theoretical real return of 0 percent against the 20 percent gross committed for. Now, in point of fact, the investor who is forever governed by the unknown deal will never invest, always fearing tomorrow might bring something better than today has offered. That investor is doomed to never earn a real return.

But, in an imperfect world of imperfect communication, the likelihood that the investor has not made the best deal must have some real effect. In a target-rich environment the effect will be greater than in a target-poor one, because the investor will be more inclined to worry about all those other targets out there.

Liquidity Preference

Related to opportunity cost, liquidity preference is the desire or need for a degree of liquidity. As more and more available capital is committed, the danger increases that there will not be enough capital to fund operations to carry the target through lean times and to make the most of good times. In other words, there is always the risk the business will be undercapitalized, and the substantial capital previously invested will be lost for want of additional backup capital.

Up to a point, there will be funds available, but at an increasingly higher cost, whether the funds are from lenders or co-investors. The impact on the current cost of capital might be quantified by considering the blended effect on the cost of capital as higher cost increments are called into play. This impact will naturally be greater as the price of the business approaches the limit of availability, because the cost of capital continuum usually will look like Figure 2.6.

Initially the real cost of capital will actually decline as more is invested, because the associated administrative costs will be greater for the smallest amounts. Beyond a certain point, the trend will reverse and cost will start

Figure 2.6: Capital Availability versus Cost of Capital

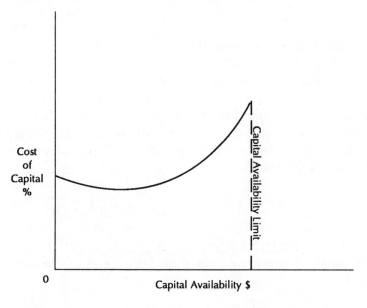

to go up, climbing at an accelerating rate as the limits of availability are reached.

Maturity

Another facet of the impact of availability on cost of capital becomes apparent when some portion of the funding must be paid back, usually at the maturity date on the loan, but possibly in a guaranteed return of capital to co-investors. The sooner repayment is required, the greater the impact on cost of capital, especially if the business will have difficulty generating enough free capital to liquidate the requirement.

The maturity demand will more greatly influence the cost of capital the further along the capital availability continuum we have advanced. As it becomes more likely the maturity need will arise at a time when capital is less available, the cost goes up.

Variability

Perhaps most obviously, probable variations in the stated cost (for example, a floating rate note) will impact the cost of capital. Variability may be produced not only by a variable interest rate formula, but also by contingencies in contracts (for example, higher payout to co-investors when certain events occur) and by foreign exchange fluctuations in cross-border investments.

Tax Status

What ultimately matters, of course, is the after-tax cost of capital versus the after-tax rate of return. The tax profile a buyer brings to the table will naturally determine the after-tax cost and rate to be realized.

The differences in cost of capital often explain how one investor may offer much more for a target than others. Of course, it's also possible their perceptions of the prospects and characteristics of the business differ. Perhaps somebody simply is mistaken. It happens to the best analysts and investors. Wall Street is full of such tales.

PROJECTIONS

Before reviewing the analytical methods for fixing a baseline value, we first must be sure the numbers—revenues, costs, profits, capital needs, asset values, and other variables—are accurate. Maybe, since we're talking about projecting the future, "realistic" is a better word than "accurate," for we'll only be able to judge accuracy in hindsight.

There are seven broad methods for selecting particular figures:

1. Replication
2. Functionates
3. Averaging
4. Probability
5. Curve fitting
6. Min–Max and simulation
7. Gut projection

Let's look at the details.

Replication

Replication presumes the future will be practically identical to the past. One interpretation is next year's revenues will be the same as this year's revenues. Or it could mean that since this year's revenues were up 5 percent over last year's, next year's will be up another 5 percent.

Though most analysts will have the reaction that replication is unsophisticated, in fact every analyst subconsciously adopts it in broad outlines by assuming (and quite rightly) at minimum past performance is indeed the launching pad for from which more sophisticated analysis may proceed.

Functionates

"Functionates" is a term of your author's creation. Though the reader may be unfamiliar with the coined word, the technique is likely to strike a responsive cord.

It presumes certain fixed relationships among different performance variables. On the P&L, the most common functionate used is revenues, with different costs projected as a percentage of revenue. Some may jump to the concluding point of profit as a fixed percent of revenue, but it is usually more realistic to project costs and then subtract from revenue to get profit. That is because some costs (rent, officer salaries, hazard insurance, depreciation, for example) will not vary with revenue and should not be projected as a percentage of it.

Put another way, functionates are a form of projection based on variable, semivariable and fixed cost classification. Here's a quick example:

The following is a summary of Sample Company's 19X7 numbers in thousands:

Account		
Total Revenues	$1,629	100.0%
Cost of Sales	1,104	67.8
Gross Profit	525	32.2
Overhead	430	26.4
Operating Profit	95	5.8
Net Interest Expense	7	0.4
Pretax Profit	88	5.4
Income Taxes	32	2.0
Net Profit	56	3.4

For the moment, next year's revenues are projected at $1,950,000. Does that mean net profit next year should be (3.4%) (1,950,000) = $66,300?

The more sophisticated (and more realistic) approach shows:

Account		
Revenues	$1,950	100.0%
Direct Expenses	1,322	67.8
Gross Profit	628	32.2
Overhead	495	25.4
Operating Profit	133	6.8
Net Interest Expense	7	0.4
Pretax Profit	126	6.4
Income Taxes	38	1.9
Net Profit	88	4.5

The overhead components have been figured offline, with some, like rent, rising very little, but others, like advertising and promotion, rising in line with sales. Note that Net Interest Expense would be figured based on the projected capital needs, while the Income Taxes are obviously a function of Pretax Profits. This little exercise merely demonstrates the power of operating leverage, but it's a point which shouldn't be missed.

Functionates are not limited to financial statements. For example, revenues may be estimated as a function of the number of locations for a retail operation or the number of salespeople on the road for a wholesaler. Similarly, health insurance costs will be a function of the number of employees; fuel costs a function of the number of vehicles.

Functionates often have their greatest utility as tests of the figures projected by other means. A sophisticated, computer-driven, statistical curve fit program (see section on Curve Fitting) that yields a projection of equipment repair costs may not stand up when tested against a functionate ratio of hours of use versus anticipated production level.

Averaging

Averaging is an almost instinctive reaction to an array of past performance numbers. The tendency to believe that numbers will fluctuate around a norm (the implicit assumption for accepting an average as valid) is often correct, particularly in the business world.

However, averages can be mighty tricky, because there are so many ways to calculate them. Should the average encompass the past 3, 5, 10, 20, or how many periods? Should the periods be months, quarters, or years? Should we average the absolute number or the rate of change? Should we use a simple average, a moving average, a weighted average, or a median? Should we drop out the high and low? Or maybe drop those outside the range of the standard deviation?

The method will most certainly determine the message. And there is no hard-and-fast rule as to when one type of average or another is the right choice. An averaging process is best used when it is rationally and explicitly justified, both in general and with regard to the specific subtechnique employed.

Probability

Probability analysis postulates a limited universe of possibilities from which the most likely figure is extracted. It is essentially another averaging technique, but one which arguably has the advantage of future orientation over mere historical averages. It is most easily explained with an example.

Say we're looking at a summer resort for blue-collar families. Our analyst projects next summer's revenues to be between $750,000 (75 percent of capacity) and $1,000,000 (100 percent of capacity). Weather is the single biggest factor in determining revenue; but the state of the economy, especially as reflected in unemployment statistics and manufacturing output, is also a determinant. After consulting weather and economic predictions, the analyst subjectively rates 5 percent capacity increments and manipulates them to a single projection:

Capacity: $1,000,000			
Capacity (%)	Revenue	Probability (%)	Product
75	750,000	10	75,000
80	800,000	25	200,000
85	850,000	30	255,000
90	900,000	20	180,000
95	950,000	10	95,000
100	1,000,000	5	50,000
Single Projection (Sum of Product)			855,000

Parenthetically we might note this kind of example is especially susceptible to this kind of analysis. It may be interpreted that over the course of the summer (reading from the bottom up) the resort will be full 5 percent of the time, 95 percent full 10 percent of the time, and so forth.

Probability analysis can be made more sophisticated by using statistical probability distributions, like the normal curve or Poisson distribution among others, to assign a probability to a given outcome. These distributions also offer internal tests for validating the fit of the method to the data. These multiple tests at increasing levels of sophistication offer greater confidence to the analyst than flat-out guesses or simple averages.

Curve Fitting

Curve fitting is also an averaging technique, albeit a sophisticated one with some of the advantages of probability analysis. It may be described as a self-projecting average as the internal mechanics of averaging may be used to project a future outcome. Curve fitting is often used to predict a variable as a function of time.

There are four typical curve equations in which a single variable is predicted as dependent upon the determining independent variable. The mathematical proofs, logic, and full explanation of these statistical methods are beyond the scope of this book. Any good elementary statistics text, such as *General Statistics* by Warren Chase and Fred Brown (John Wiley & Sons, 1986) will explain them. The easiest way, though, to take advantage of this method is to use one of the many statistical computer software packages available. Even some preprogrammed scientific and business calculators offer these statistical functions.

For the record, the four equations are:

Linear: $y = a + (b)(x)$

Exponential: $y = (a)(e)^{(b)(x)}$ $(a > 0)$

Logarithmic: $y = a + (b)(\ln x)$

Power: $y = (a)(x)^b$ $(a > 0)$

Data can, of course, be plugged into any one of the four, but the key to the method is a follow-up formula that measures fit. The output is the correlation coefficient, which will have a value between 0.0 (no fit) and 1.0 (perfect fit). The correlation formula is fairly complex, but is a part of any statistical computer package. Its symbol is r.

Let's look at an example. (This one was worked out using a Hewlett-Packard programmable calculator.) Say we want to see which curve provides the best fit for seven years of Sample's gross sales (in 000's) using time as the independent variable:

Year	Time = x	Sales = y
19X1	1	1008
19X2	2	949
19X3	3	894
19X4	4	900
19X5	5	1193
19X6	6	1350
19X7	7	1629
Totals	28	7923

The results produced, including projections for the next five years under each curve, are:

Result	Linear	Expon.	Log.	Power	Average of 4
r	0.83	0.82	0.66	0.65	0.74
a	708428	780980	808598	849075	
b	105857	0.09	265319	0.22	
19X8	1555285	1564788	1360314	1332630	1453254
19X9	1661142	1706799	1391564	1367093	1531650
19Y0	1767000	1861699	1419518	1398675	1611723
19Y1	1872857	2030656	1444806	1427873	1694048
19Y2	1978714	2214947	1467892	1455061	1779154

From the correlation coefficient (*r*) we can see that the linear curve has the best fit, though an exponential curve is only marginally inferior. Even the other two methods are not statistically unreliable; they're just not the best we're able to compute. However, since those two are substantially less reliable than the first two, and give substantially different projections, we'll be more likely to use linear or exponential in the calculations.

Figure 2.7 shows a graph of the four curves plotted against the actual numbers through 19X7, and the forecasts plotted into the next five years, against the simple average of the four, which itself may be useful as a range-narrowing predictor.

Checking the other key summary numbers, Cost of Sales and Overhead, not surprisingly, they too are good linear fits, having coefficients of 0.81 and 0.91 respectively. (Overhead had a slightly better exponential fit at 0.93. However, intuitively, if overhead grows exponentially while sales, direct costs, and thus gross profit grow linearly, the business will fail once overhead exceeds gross profit, as losses would be projected forever. An owner will control overhead if it begins to run amok.)

One curious point about all the projections, including the linear projection: They all show a *drop* in sales for at least a year. The latter two don't even catch up to the old level in five years. Using the linear best fit, we must ask ourselves if that is reasonable. If the business changes hands, would it mean a pruning back until the new owners get settled in? Is there economic trouble these statistics are mirroring?

In fact, as wonderful as these statistics are, they are *just* statistics. It happens to be the way the numbers work out, but it still deserves attention, because it indicates some historical difficulty, which we can see easily in the falling sales (and net losses) in the 19X1 to 19X3 period. Perhaps Sample is cyclical and our statistical efforts have stumbled on that fact. We'll have to look deeper into the question and be more wary about our projections.

Min–Max and Simulation

Min–Max and Simulation allows there is no single answer and prefers to think in terms of ranges rather than pinpoints. There is much to be said in favor of such a humbly realistic approach to the future.

Min—Max looks simultaneously at the best possible, worst possible, and most likely outcomes. (Best and worst are not open-ended, but rather lie within the realm of reasonable expectation.) Hence it may be more appropriate to call it Min–Likely–Max.

Simulation goes one step further and considers many, or even all, the reasonably possible combinations of factors that will yield a bottom line.

Figure 2.7: Sales Projections Using Curve Fit Formulas

(000's)

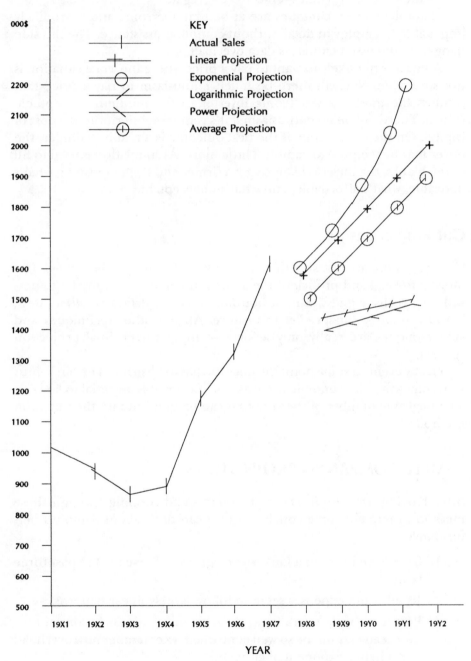

These may be ordered from worst to best to give the analyst the full panorama of the range. The outcomes are also susceptible to all the averaging techniques, but even more useful may be a scatter diagram to see where the bulk of outcomes tends to congregate.

Naturally these techniques are at best cumbersome and more likely impossible to employ in detail without computer assistance. The flip side danger, as discussed earlier, is data overload.

A buyer is not likely to want to pay a price where the worst situation is not survivable. Nor will there be much enthusiasm to pay a price that renders the most likely outcome inferior to the minimum acceptable return. There will be no enthusiasm if it's rendered inferior to the cost of capital. On the other hand, if the best outcome is a real humdinger, the buyer may be tempted to gamble a little more. As simulation is used to fill in the blanks, the buyer is likely to get a firmer and firmer grasp on what's desirable, what's affordable, and what's unacceptable.

Gut Projections

Gut projections are just what they sound like—the analyst's best guess. The more informed and proficient the analyst, the more likely the best guess will be a realistic guess. But, at bottom, every projection is *only* a guess, because nobody can predict the future. All the other techniques and subtechniques are really only a form of input to the final projection (guess).

In any event, at some point the decision has to be made. The buck must stop somewhere if economic progress is to occur. It is essential to land on a manageable number of statistics that can be plugged into the valuation methods.

SAMPLE COMPANY'S PROJECTIONS

After looking over the financial statements and running through these methods, there are some conclusions we can draw about Sample's performance:

1. Sales have been on a fairly steady growth course for the past three years.
2. Its sales and expenses seem to follow largely linear patterns.
3. Profits are rather erratic, while gross margin is fairly constant, so overhead may not be so well controlled. (Remember how overhead had a better exponential curve fit?)

4. The growth area in sales has been on the service end of the business.

5. The business is not highly leveraged.

Taking these factors into account, we might project steady, but not spectacular, growth in sales, a constant gross profit, and slower growth in overhead. The last of these points is assumed with some risk, because the history of the firm exhibits difficulty in controlling overhead. Our deal completion bias may be impelling us to make that assumption, but we will test it later on. So, we'll make these 10-year projections:

Sales Growth = 10% per year.

Gross Profit = 31% (cost of sales is 69%) close to both 7- *and* 3-year averages.

Overhead = 8% per year increase, a slower rate than sales growth.

Net Interest Expense = 0.5% of sales.

Taxes = Combined average rate of 35% of pretax profits.

The actual projections based on these assumptions are contained in Appendix 1.

READY TO GO

Having completed the work described so far, we can be confident of several things:

1. We're satisfied we've collected adequate, timely, and reasonably accurate data.

2. We've got a handle on our financial objective in terms of rate of return and its subsidiary elements of stream-of-income and capital appreciation.

3. We've evaluated our resources and determined our cost of capital and the contingent influences on it, including variability, opportunity cost, liquidity, maturity, and tax status.

4. We've determined how we want to project the future and what we see as the range and likelihood, within that range of the business's output.

Hence, we're ready to put some hard numbers together to come up with a baseline price for the target company.

Chapter 3

Financial Framework

Finding the Clinical Baseline Value

OBJECTIVE

The purpose we focus on here is to establish a purely clinical value for the business. In a sense, we're seeking a norm. This single price will usually be found to be some kind of magnet:

1. A floor below which offers to sellers are likely to be summarily rejected;
2. A ceiling above which no offers from buyers can be expected; or
3. A median value around which offers tend to congregate.

The fact a particular value turns out to be one or another of these is not a reflection on the analyst, but rather on the nature of the business and the circumstances of the marketplace at the time.

A business in a growing field which is seen as not yet having achieved its full potential is likely to find the clinical value establishing a floor, especially if the economy is strong and the capital markets are easy. Conversely, a mature business in a declining industry will more likely find the clinical value is a ceiling value, especially when the economy is weak and money is tight.

It's also fair to say that there's no single "automatic" clinical value. Rather, because there are a number of mathematical methods (which we will be exploring very shortly) a degree of opinion and judgment must be relied on in deciding which to favor, or how to weight them, or where, within the range they establish, the analyst should land. Let's look at the choices.

METHODS

Each of the methods for a clinical determination fall into one of four categories of methodology:

1. Asset Values
2. Stream-of-Income Values
3. Combination Methods
4. Marketplace Methods

Asset Values

Asset Values focus exclusively on the balance sheet, tending therefore to limit analysis to the present state of the business, without particular regard for the prospects of the business. Though one may well argue such an approach is shortsighted, there are several counterarguments. The most powerful, but not necessarily persuasive, argument is that prediction of the future is always subject to debate and manipulation, while the current state of a business can accurately be assessed.

Hence, asset values are popular in transactions among existing owners, such as between partners or in sales of stock to employees. They also make obvious sense where the fundamentals of the business are asset oriented. The purest example is a mutual fund whose value is a function of the securities it owns at the moment of valuation.

Stream-of-Income Values

Stream-of-Income Values focus exclusively on the profit-and-loss statement, tending therefore to limit analysis to future prospects with somewhat less attention to the present state of the business.

These methods are most applicable to industries in which hard assets play a minor role, industries that instead are dominated by their labor component. These industries often are characterized by ease of entry and concommitant fragmentation. Consulting firms, advertising agencies, brokers of all sorts, and professional practices are prime examples of the businesses where these methods may be applied without substantial criticism.

Combination Methods

Combination Methods are, not surprisingly, either hybrids of the first two types of methods, or are based on an integration of the two types. Also not surprisingly, they would seem to be those that should be most widely used.

However, because combinations are more complex, they are also more open to attack on the grounds they require too many assumptions, and even may be unnecessarily complicated, without producing a more reliable result. These arguments generally will not be persuasive, but they are worth remembering when testing results.

Combination methods are, nevertheless, worth examining for the widest range of business types, as so many industries find both assets and labor capable of materially affecting operating results.

Marketplace Methods

Marketplace Methods are the fourth category and differ wholly in perspective from the first three. Asset, Stream-of-Income and Combination Methods are all internally oriented, with self-generated financial statistics as the engine of determination.

By contrast, Marketplace Methods draw their power from comparisons. Consequently, like Combinations, they too are broadly applicable. Yet, criticism may be well founded on the grounds that the concept of valuation without regard for those internal statistics is inconsistent with logic. Furthermore, the vagaries of the marketplace may perpetuate an unrealistic or distorted approach, especially as these methods tend to be strongly influenced by industry factors. If there's a flaw in the basis of comparison that is employed, the flaw will be incorporated in the result.

Still, because the perspective is so different, they make a wonderful contrapuntal test of the other three classes. Beware, though, for there may not always be adequate or reliable comparisons available.

The utility of these methods can be portrayed with this schematic:

Figure 3.1: Schematic Valuation Methods Utility

Asset-Based   Labor-Based

Mutual Funds Natural Resources Real Estate Financial Insurance	Manufacturers Transportation Utilities Restaurants Distributors Retailers Media	Professionals Consultants Brokers Services
Asset Value Methods Apply	Combination Methods Apply	Stream-of-Income Methods Apply

— — — — — — — Marketplace Methods Apply — — — — — —

The examples are not cited for the purpose of pigeonholing into a method category, but to indicate the kinds of businesses most likely to be amenable to a particular category of methods. Hence, a software consulting firm that owns prime real estate and holds several valuable copyrights may be more fairly priced with an asset emphasis. On the other hand, an oil company with largely played-out wells, but with exceptional brokering and marketing abilities, may be more properly priced with an earnings emphasis.

These points may logically lead to the conclusion that only in rare circumstances will it be wise to limit oneself to a single class of methods, or even to fewer than all four classes. It is recommended that at least passing consideration be given to the whole panoply.

The classes contain the following specific methods:

ASSET-BASED METHODS

Book Value	Adjusted Book Value	Present Net Asset Growth Value
Replacement Value		Startup Value

STREAM-OF-INCOME METHODS

Payback	Income Ratio Value	Rate of Return	Discounted Income Value

COMBINATION METHODS

Excess Income Plus Assets	Total Present Value

MARKETPLACE METHODS

Prior Sales	Comparison Values	Market to Book	Revenue Multiplier

tance of the books at face value. From the standing start of Book Value (still referring to the 19X7 Sample Company Balance Sheet) following are the questions, with sample answers, to get to Adjusted Book Value (ABV):

ABV Main Question #1: Which assets should be revised in value and by how much?

On the Current Asset level these are the subsidiary questions for the accounts:

Cash & Equivalents: Have any securities in the "equivalents" changed a lot in value from what is shown in the books? It is rarely worth considering unless the securities are equities or have maturities at least a year out, as the changes are not likely to be material otherwise. We find none for Sample Company.

Accounts Receivable: Are the Bad Debt Reserves accurate? At minimum, the analyst needs to see an Aging Schedule. Some may think it's a minimal issue, but do a majority of the customers take a prompt payment discount? Sample's terms are 2/10, Net 30, and half the accounts pay promptly, so that's a 1 percent move on receivables. In Sample's case, receivables are the largest single account, and 1 percent is material in overall dollars. Additionally, a $12,000 account is being carried on the books, but the customer filed for bankruptcy. So we find a *downward* adjustment of:

$$(1\%)(202,740 - 12,000) + 12,000 = \$13,907.$$

Inventory: Two things for the analyst to do here. First, walk through and *see* the inventory. Get a feel for condition, care in storage, packaging, waste, and, most importantly, the personnel handling the stuff. If inventory is kept in several locations, ideally see them all, but at least see enough to be confident of the company's standard. From the seller's standpoint, the exercise is still applicable to internalize a buyer's perspective, to look for places to improve salability, and to find, perhaps, some new operating improvements in case the business doesn't sell.

Secondly, *see* the inventory records, especially the physical count, extension, and reconciliation to the books. If no count has been taken recently, take one. "Recently" will depend on the business. A broader product line, a higher inventory turnover rate, a larger number of locations, a history of disparity between physical and book, or an inventory representing a higher percentage of assets will all incline toward "recently" meaning not more than just a month or two ago.

For the purposes of Adjusted Book Value, look for soft spots in the inventory, meaning items which should be written down, written off or are missing.

Review of Sample's inventory yields several candidates for writeoff due to obsolescence, totalling $6,000, and a historical 2 percent damage and pilferage adjustment. The result is another *downward* adjustment of

$$\$6,000 + (2\%)(72746 - 6000) = \$7335$$

Miscellaneous Receivables: What are they? Any time the word "Miscellaneous" shows up, the question must be raised as to just what it stands for.

For Sample, it turns out they're accounts labeled "Due from Employees," "Due from Officers," and "Local Tax Refunds Receivable." No cause for change.

Prepaid Expenses: What are these? Any sort of capitalized expenses (another good example is Research & Development Costs on the Balance Sheet) are suspect as a source of value, because they represent money already spent. Unless there is some salable asset left from the exercise, and one that will remain salable at the point ownership of the business transfers, these expenses shouldn't be included toward arriving at a price under this method.

Sample's Prepaid Expenses represent insurance premiums. Those will shortly be expensed. *Reduce* assets by $8267.

While most adjustments on the Current Assets level tend to be downward, Fixed Assets often offer opportunity for increments, though decreases can show up, too.

Real Estate: Realty and its products (minerals, fossil fuels, timber, for example) are often the source of the largest writeups, because accounting rules (depreciation and depletion) work down the value on the books based on original cost, while market values of the assets frequently are rising.

That is the situation with Sample. The present Fair Market Value (FMV) of the real estate is $150,000. Hence, there's an *addition* of:

FMV	–	Book Cost	+	Accumulated Deprec.	=	Increment
$150,000	–	105,982	+	89,115	=	$133,133

Equipment and Fixtures: If there is to be an adjustment on these accounts (and often there will be) it's usually because book depreciation does not track real market value. If fully depreciated assets remain in service, there quite clearly will be an understatement.

But assets can be found to be overstated, especially if concentrated in an area of rapidly changing technology, which tends to more quickly make existing equipment obsolete. All sorts of electronic equipment seem predisposed to this risk.

Just like product inventories, the inventory of equipment should be seen in person and the records (especially specifications and maintenance) should be reviewed in detail. Sample's equipment inventory is a mixed bag, looking like this:

	FMV	–	Book	+	Accum. Deprec.	=	Increment
Computer System	$3,000	–	20,000	+	15,960	=	–$1,040
Test Equipment	$8,000	–	20,000	+	14,000	=	$2,000
Manufacturing Equipment	$41,000	–	60,000	+	50,000	=	$31,000
Furn. & Fixtures	$3,000	–	8,835	+	8,835	=	$3,000
Totals	$55,000	–	108,835	+	88,795	=	$34,960

A net *upward* adjustment of $34,960.

Vehicles: Vehicles really are just another form of the equipment story. It is worthwhile for the analyst to keep in mind that vehicles are notorious for losing economic value rapidly, so a relatively newer fleet is likely to be subject to greater writedowns for Adjusted Book. On the other hand, vehicles can last longer than the fairly short depreciation periods commonly used, so an older than normal fleet may get written up. Sample's vehicle account is fully depreciated, but has a salvage market value to be added in of $1,000.

Miscellaneous Assets usually include intangible assets, but may occasionally contain some tangibles. Many intangibles are especially hard to get a handle on. To take some extreme cases, what's the Coca-Cola trademark worth? How about the copyrights on the Disney film library? Or the patent on any wonder drug? Even more common intangibles on the books like franchise fees, licenses, customer lists, and goodwill (from prior acquisitions) are hard to deal with. What is particularly tough about them is they all beg the question of the overall value of the business.

Some intangible values may be quite volatile. A patent may suddenly be superseded by a competitor's technology. A license may suddenly be worthless because of deregulation.

Sample's life insurance policy's cash value is indisputable. The patent is another story. The FMV of a patent should be equal to the present value of the incremental net revenues (whether from product sales, patent licensing agreements, or sale of the patent rights) it's expected to generate. We'll explore some of the finer points of Present Value calculations later on. For now, suffice it to say Sample's patent has an estimated current value of $25,000, resulting in one more *increment*:

FMV	–	Book Cost	+	Accum. Amortiz.	=	Increment
$25,000	–	17,000	+	7,000	=	$15,000

ABV Main Question #2: Are there any assets not on the balance sheet that should be included?

Such items are almost always intangibles of one sort or another. Here's a checklist of such items:

Trade secrets	Tax refunds due
Customer lists	Overfunded pension plan
Mailing lists	Proprietary processes
Vendor lists	Customer contracts
Patent licenses	Leasehold rights
Proprietary formulas	Chattel lease rights
Employment contracts	Regulatory licenses
Government contracts	

Three tangible areas that may yield some additions are:

Accounts Receivable Writeoffs: Are there accounts that have been written off but are in fact collectible, perhaps in part? That is not uncommon with customer bankruptcies, as most vendors write off the account upon notice, even though a partial payoff may arise from the bankruptcy.

Inventory Writeoffs: Are there inventory items written off that are still salable? (N.B.: Changes in tax regulations for writeoffs now make the likelihood small. If assets are found, their incremental value may be offset by a corresponding back tax liability.)

Depreciated Equipment: While equipment still in use should stay on the balance sheet (offset by the accumulated depreciation) smaller outfits with less sophisticated accounting abilities sometimes remove them. The potential increment is the real value of those fully depreciated items.

The valuation of all of these items, especially the intangibles, may be open to some speculation. Conservative values are usually preferred.

Assume Sample leases 10,000 square feet of warehouse space for $10 per square foot, with the right to sublease. The lease still has five years to run. Current market conditions would require a tenant to spend $12 per square foot for the same space. Sample has recently been offered a $25,000 premium to sublease, which it rejected.

The premium could be included in making the adjustments to book value, but the analyst should be wary here. If we're seeking to liquidate the company, that sort of asset has a value. But in this case, with the company needing the space (or something comparable) the premium isn't going to be realized and will eventually be dissipated as the lease term winds down.

ABV Main Question #3: Which liabilities should be revised in value and by how much?

Accounts Payable should be looked at to be sure disputed accounts, discounts, and the like are not distorted or misrepresented in the balance sheet. Watch out especially for smaller companies that make only an annual adjustment to the accounts payable balance, carrying the latest year-end figure until the end of next year without change. We'll assume Sample's figures are OK.

Accrued Taxes and Expenses: Each type of tax accrual has to be reviewed. There are really two elements to accrual. One is the current liability, which is fairly easy to pinpoint. The second, which is often harder to pin down, is back taxes, including potential penalties and interest, which may become due through audit.

Accrued miscellaneous expenses are also hard for an outsider to guess at if not already accounted for, as they are usually the product of a contractual agreement. Only a thorough review of operations can ferret them out. For our example, again assume Sample has done an adequate accounting job.

Bank Debt and Mortgage Payable: Both follow the debt instruments and should be straightforward. However, if the payments are infrequent (annually, for example) or the promissory notes are in arrears (a critical point to examine in a bail-out deal) the books might not adequately recognize accrued interest, or late charges.

Another potential factor arises when the target is paying a loan carrying an interest rate substantially above the current market. A buyer may be very inclined to pay the loan off or refinance it. If the loan carries a prepayment penalty or a Rule-of-78's clause, the additional cost should be added in to the unpaid balance.

Assume Sample's bank debt is a revolving line with an annual "clean-up" requirement. Right now there's accrued interest of $500 to be *added* in.

ABV Main Question #4: Are there any liabilities not on the balance sheet that should be added in?

Liabilities in this category usually are contingent in some respect. The amounts included for analytical purposes should, however, reflect only net figures. For example, Sample is defendant in a $100,000 products liability lawsuit, but it is insured for 100 percent after a $5,000 deductible. So only $5,000 would be added into the liabilities.

A somewhat more common unstated (or understated) liability is an unfunded pension liability. Any time a target has a pension or deferred compensation plan, its integrity must be examined. It turns out Sample has a $55,000 unfunded liability.

ABV Main Question #5: Are there any liability or equity accounts that should be reclassified?

It is not uncommon to find stockholders loaning money to a company, particularly when it is closely held. Often these "loans" are a proxy for a part of the equity investment, classified on the books as loans because there are usually tax advantages to their being treated as debt. Conversely, where there are several shareholders, one or more may be in a position to demand or receive a cash buyout of equity in certain circumstances. Then the equity has what amounts to a preferential position with a claim on assets and might as well be treated as debt for purposes of valuation, especially if the preferred shareholder will be troublesome in closing a deal.

In the publicly held sector, convertible debt, preferred stock (both straight and convertible), warrants, rights, and even different classes of common stock can muddle the picture. For now, Sample apparently has no such mixed accounts.

All right, it's time to recap the numbers:

Book Value Per Balance Sheet		$297,760
Asset Changes:		
Accounts Receivable	−13,907	
Inventory	−7,335	
Prepaid Expenses	−8,267	
Real Estate	+133,133	
Equipment	+34,960	
Vehicles	+1,000	
Patent	+15,000	
Add: Total Net Asset Changes		+154,584
Liability & Equity Changes:		
Accrued Interest on Bank Debt	+500	
Lawsuit Deductible	+5,000	
Unfunded Pension Liability	+55,000	
Less: Total Liability Changes		−60,500
Adjusted Book Value		$391,844
Percentage Above or Below Stated Book Value:	+31.60%	

This significant difference in the two Book Value figures (unadjusted and adjusted) has to have a correspondingly significant impact on pricing and negotiations.

Book Value and Adjusted Book Value concentrate on the current state of the business. They force the buyer to focus only on paying a fair price for what's being obtained today.

Present Net Asset Growth Value

Present Net Asset Growth Value concentrates instead on the future state of the business. The buyer's focus is on what's going to be obtained when the buyer turns into a seller at some point in the future. (We could also call this method Present Net Worth Growth Value.)

Three factors go into the calculation: (1) The Time Period, (2) The Growth Rate, (3) The Discount Rate.

The Time Period: How long until the buyer plans to sell? We'll assume 10 years for purposes of illustration.

The Growth Rate: How fast will the Net Assets grow? One approach to answering that question is to make a seat-of-the-pants estimate.

A better approach is to look at the historical rate of growth. The end-point rate for Sample (19X1 to 19X7) has been roughly 11.25 percent compounded. The 7-year period would be computed from the beginning of 19X1 when equity stood as:

$$\text{Closing Equity} - \text{19X1 Profits} = \text{Opening Equity}$$

$$\$182,654 \quad - \quad 41,403 \quad = \quad \$141,251.$$

(As we're seeking the opening figure for 19X1, the profit of $41,403 earned during the year 19X1 is subtracted.) The end of 19X7 showed a net worth of $297,760. To get from $141, 251 to $297,760 in seven years is a compound rate of growth of 11.242 percent, which we'll conveniently round up to 11.25 percent.

Therefore, in 10 years, assuming that rate of growth is sustained, Net Assets will nearly triple:

$$(1.1125)^{10} = 2.904$$

The Discount Rate: The third factor should equal the minimum rate of return on investment the buyer finds acceptable. By using such a discount rate, the buyer is able to derive an acceptable price to pay today for that value to be realized in the future. Let's assume a minimum of 15 percent.

The formula for the calculation is:

$$\frac{(1 + G)^n A}{(1 + i)^n}$$

where: n = Number of Years, G = Growth Rate, i = Discount Rate, A = Net Assets at time of analysis.

Plugging the Book Value figures in, we get a strange result:

$$\frac{(1 + 11.25\%)^{10}(297,760)}{(1 + 15\%)^{10}}$$

$$\frac{864,702}{4.05}$$

$$= \$213,741!!!!$$

Because the Discount Rate exceeds the Growth Rate, the result is to recommend a price below Book Value. That's an irrational result, because we could presumably buy the business for $213,741 and turn right around and resell for Book Value of $297,760. Hence, this approach must sometimes default back to the Book Value employed in the formula.

In this particular example, though, it may be wiser to use Adjusted Book Value, in which case the Growth Rate (from $141,251 to $391,844) over the seven years has been 15.69 percent. Then we'll end up with a small premium over Adjusted Book Value, because 15.69 percent is greater than 15 percent:

$$\frac{(1 + .1569)^{10}\,(391,844)}{(1.15)^{10}}$$

$$= \$416,000$$

True, we may be mixing apples and oranges if Book Value and Adjusted Book Value were not equal at the starting point. That's one of the method's pitfalls. It's important to keep in mind the increase or decrease ultimately realized, will be a function of the profits and losses rolling into the equity account. So this is one Balance Sheet oriented method overcoming (at least indirectly) the chief criticism of asset-based valuations as not considering future prospects.

Replacement Value

Replacement Value asks "How much would it cost to duplicate the essential features of this business from scratch?" Replacement Value may be equivalent to the Fair Market Value of the assets, which means it will be the same as Adjusted Book Value. On the other hand, it may be well nigh impossible to find equipment, facilities, and the like of the same age and condition. Furthermore, it may not make sense to duplicate all the assets as they exist, but rather to duplicate their function. This distinction from Adjusted Book Value is a subtle one, and in many cases it may be a distinction without a difference. But it can also be a powerful concept, for if duplicating the business will be significantly less expensive, the buyer may prefer to do just that. Or, if duplication will now be a lot more expensive, the buyer may have a powerful incentive to pay a hefty premium over Adjusted Book Value.

A simple example involves a printing company with several older presses. Technology has advanced to the point where all the presses could be *replaced* by a single press with equal or greater production capacity. Replacement also offers the benefits of requiring less labor and permitting occupancy of smaller, and thus less expensive, facilities, without sacrificing any revenues at all. If the seller insists on getting the going price for the old presses as part of the business price, it may be a very tough sell.

Replacement Value mandates the same line-item review as Adjusted Book Value. Looking at Sample, we find:

Cash and Accounts Receivable: These (less Bad Debts) are effectively equal to Working Capital. From a Replacement Value standpoint, how much do we need to operate? A simple approximation would be to take average total expenses during an Accounts Receivable cycle. If the average age of receivables is 45 days, or 1.5 months, we need

$$(1.5/12) \text{ (Annual Expenses)}$$

$$(1.5/12)(\text{Purchases} + \text{Direct} + \text{Overhead} + \text{Interest}) = \text{Needs}$$

$$(0.125)(361,946 + 758,855 + 429,536 + 9,651) = \$194,998$$

Call it $200,000 to give us a little cushion.

Inventory: What's the market value of the inventory? What would it cost to replace? (Remember, we're not talking about retail sale value, but rather the cost to have the product "on the shelf" ready for sale.) If the inventory is accounted for on a Last-In, First-Out basis, or if inventory turnover is slow, the likelihood is high that Replacement Value will differ from Book; most often, inflation means it will differ by being higher. But the dross in inventory has to be weeded out.

Assume a look at Sample's inventory shows replacement cost is 15 percent more than the Balance Sheet figure. Taking out the writedowns (See Adjusted Book Value) we find:

$$(1.15\%)(72,746 - 7335) = \$75,223$$

Let's round down to $75,000.

Miscellaneous Receivables: Those employee advances aren't essential; forget about them.

Prepaid Expenses: The insurance premiums are going to be necessary, though they may be examined to be sure all the coverages are needed and the limits acceptable. Assume no changes, leaving a figure of $8,267.

Real Estate: From Adjusted Book Value calculations, we know the Fair

Market Value of the realty is $150,000. As long as the facilities are sufficient and there's no surplus space, stick with the number.

Equipment and Fixtures and Vehicles: When stripped to essentials and priced new these would cost $160,000 to replace.

Miscellaneous Assets: The life insurance is not essential, so it's zero for these purposes. The patent technology has largely been supplanted in the marketplace by another, which can be acquired for a nominal fee. That cost is effectively covered by our Working Capital cushion, so this asset can also be zeroed.

Adding up these asset figures and subtracting the statement liabilities:

Working Capital	$200,000
Inventory	75,000
Miscellaneous Receivables	0
Prepaid Expenses	8,267
Real Estate	150,000
Equipment, Fixtures & Vehicles	160,000
Miscellaneous Assets	0
Total Assets Replacement Value	593,267
Less: Total Liabilities	−114,023
Replacement Value	$479,244

What this method tends to overlook are many of the intangibles—management, staff, reputation and going concern value—which may be the keys to profitability. It is also criticized as requiring far too much subjectivity. Indeed, it arguably converts the business for sale into an imaginary business bearing only a faint resemblance to the real item.

Startup Value

So maybe a buyer ought to consider a somewhat different, but related, alternative like starting a brand new business identical to the one on the block. Startup Value answers the question, "What would it cost to set up an equivalent business?"

In a real sense, considering Startup is a form of the financial analyst's well known "make versus buy" decision. From this perspective, two implicit assumptions must be true for the analysis to be realistic:

1. The market is large enough, given extant competition, to accommodate another player.
2. The full necessary range of resources is available to form a startup operation.

If the first assumption is not true, it may imply that an existing company has a greater intangible value because of its established presence. On the other hand, it may signal a limited, declining, or saturated market, which would denigrate value.

Startup Value puts a ceiling on price, because if the business can be successfully duplicated at a lower price, why pay more? One must be sure, however, the Startup is more than just entry into the industry, but, in fact, will be a comparable company.

Calculation is very similar to Replacement Value, but there are some differences, which amount to a freer form approach. For example, might the facilities or some or all of the equipment be leased instead of purchased? If feasible, the up-front cash requirements are substantially reduced, as are capital carrying costs like interest. Since realty leases are usually much shorter than building life, even when the lease amount is capitalized, the value tends to be lower. Even equipment leases may yield a lower line-item balance, if the residual value of the lease will be retained by the lessor and therefore not capitalized. Similarly, it is possible lower inventories may be workable and some of the excess can be jettisoned to further reduce working capital needs.

If all that is true, one might ask, "Why bother with Replacement Value?" The answer is Replacement Value takes the business as it now exists and manipulates it, while Startup Value is really testing for an alternative. In economic terms, the Startup Value substitute offers a reference price.

While those factors of leasing, inventory cutback, overhead reduction, and capital carrying cost reduction are cutting price, the intangibles of management, staff, reputation, tradename, and the like are pushing it up. So do the miscellaneous costs of setup, which include expenses like licensing, moving, hiring, and installation. Startup may mean deposits with vendors. It almost certainly will require greater promotional expenses. And it may mean a higher aggregate cost of capital, because lenders and investors are likely to view a startup as a riskier proposition.

While all these positive and negative factors can be estimated, we're not going to do it for Sample. It is so well established in its market and its field that a new competitor just isn't going to be able to acquire the reputation for dependability. In other words, "goodwill" may mean much more than just an accounting entry.

It is fair to say the younger the business and the greater the ease of entry; the more fragmented the industry and the lesser the personnel skill levels required, then the more sense it makes to consider Startup Value. If one wants pancakes, most any cook will do. If one desires crepes, it takes a chef.

OTHER ASSET-BASED METHODS

Three other Asset-Based Methods are well-known, but are applicable only in limited situations:

Liquidation Value is similar to Adjusted Book Value, but considers the worth of the assets in the light of a liquidation—a close-down—of the business. (Of course, liabilities are calculated for payoff.) Without the going concern value and with the expectation of rapid sale, (perhaps at an auction) because the company will not be maintaining an infrastructure to support the assets, Liquidation Value is usually the lowest assignable value. It is not normally used in valuations for sales and purchases because it presumes an end to the business, not a continuation.

Tangible Book Value is also an offshoot of Adjusted Book Value, but doesn't include any value for intangible assets. The operative theory is that intangibles are too speculative to receive an ongoing concrete value and so the conservative approach is to value only the tangible assets which can be seen, felt, and possessed in physical terms. In fact, this is a rather outmoded view, dating back to the time when many of today's very valuable intangibles—franchises, registered trademarks, regulatory licenses, tax benefits, data banks, etc.—were unknown. Tangible Book also yields a low-end value by virtue of its exclusionary approach.

Fair Market Assets is also similar to, and may be identical to, Adjusted Book Value. It treats each asset separately and asks what it would fetch if sold separately. Like Liquidation Value, it presumes no going concern value in the asset, but it doesn't presume a fire sale, dump-at-any-price viewpoint. It is useful only in those situations where a buyer is seeking to break up the business and sell off its assets at a profit over cost. Fair Market Assets Value should not be confused with Break-Up Value which seeks to value a business based on fracturing it into smaller businesses (e.g., its operating divisions) which might then be sold off individually. To get a Break-Up Value, each of the components must be fully evaluated as a separate business, with the values summed, and adjusted for liabilities.

STREAM-OF-INCOME BASED METHODS

Before computing a value on a Stream-of-Income basis, it's fundamental to define and calculate to what the essential income is equal. Earlier in this chapter, the many different forms of income were included in a checklist, from which the evaluator might choose.

Earnings, cash flow, and payouts (dividends, distributions, owner salaries, and so on) all matter. Which should be most important? That depends on the analyst's goals.

Earnings will likely be most important to outsiders, like bankers, creditors, and insurors; since earnings are the most common index of value, especially for publicly held companies. Passive investors will tend to be similarly inclined.

Active investors and managers may care most about cash flow, especially if the purchase will be financed in part by others, as debt service isn't paid with earnings but with cash. Additionally, cash flow may be important as a source of funding for other activities.

Payout will obviously matter to all owners. Owner-managers may also measure payout in terms of salary, fringes, and perks, in addition to dividends (or other distributions on equity). In point of fact, the correct valuation of salary and the like should include in the Stream of Income only the excess above what would be paid to an employee to handle the job—even the job of chief executive officer. Buyers have been known to delude themselves on this issue, even to the point of "subsidizing" the company by taking less in salary than an outsider would receive. Obviously any such deficit should decrement the Stream of Income for purposes of valuation.

One other matter here: taxes. Generally, after-tax calculations (after-tax from the standpoint of the business, not the investor) are the most relied upon. However, there are a few situations where pretax numbers may be more appropriate:

1. If the tax situation for the business is so complex earning power is obscured.

2. If the form of the business may change to an untaxed status (as to the entity) such as a partnership or S corporation.

3. Where only a part of a company (for example, a division) is being sold, so that the tax burden would be artificially allocated, probably misleading the analyst.

In these cases, of course, one should project the future tax burden, just as other elements of performance will be projected. Since tax laws may change (and have changed with unsettling frequency since the mid-1970s) it may be misleading to make a decision heavily reliant on the tax treatment.

It may be wisest to examine both pretax and after-tax figures to get a feel for the "quality" of earnings, cash flow, and payout ability. For the sake of brevity, our examples of Stream-of-Income methodology will focus strictly on net after-tax earnings.

Payback

Payback looks at how long it's going to take to recover the investment on a simple dollar-for-dollar basis. Payback is more commonly used as a rule of thumb for project expenditures, where cost is pre-established, but it can be momentarily turned on its head to help in pricing a business.

First, the Payback period is established, meaning the outside time to get the investment back. If five years is chosen, the sum of the 5-year projections will equal the payback price.

Looking at our Projections from Appendix 1 for the next five years gives us profits that look like this:

5-Year Payback Value		
Year #	Year #	Net Profit
1	19X8	$53,699
2	19X9	65,099
3	19Y0	78,122
4	19Y1	92,968
5	19Y2	109,863
5-Year Payback Value:		$399,751

Of course, if a different projection method, yielding different projections, is used, a different Payback Value will result.

The criticisms of Payback are obvious. It doesn't look beyond recovery of the investment. It doesn't look beyond the arbitrary payback period. It doesn't consider the time value of money. It doesn't account for risk. Still, it is in a sense a measure of affordability and provides a dimension with some merit for any buyer with less than unlimited resources.

Income Ratio and Rate of Return

The ratio here is price to income. It is best known by the name Price–Earnings Ratio (PE). It postulates the price of the business should be a fixed multiple of earnings. (Usually the latest earnings are used.) The reciprocal of PE is the Capitalization Rate, which divides earnings by a fixed percentage.

Whichever way the fraction is played, it is a very unsophisticated formula. Nonetheless, it is widely followed, as it does provide a basis for comparison among alternatives, particularly where the companies are in the same industry. The operative theory is that the business should be throwing off enough income to provide the Capitalization Rate as a simple Rate of Return on the investment.

The "Cap" rate then should reflect the Rate of Return required by the buyer. Of course, such a rate must be above the Cost of Capital to make the purchase profitable for the buyer.

If Sample's buyer is looking for a 15 percent Rate of Return, the simplest approach is to use the latest earnings:

$$\frac{\$56,671}{.15} = \$377,807$$

Obviously, this result is the same as a PE of 6.66.

Discounted Income Value

Discounted Income Value assumes a stream of profits (or other income form) and computes an aggregate present value of the stream, which thereby considers the time value of money. The formula:

$$\frac{x_1}{(1 + i)^1} + \frac{x_2}{(1 + i)^2} + \ldots + \frac{x_n}{(1 + i)^n} = DIV$$

where:

$$x_n = \text{profit for year } n$$

$$i = \text{discount rate}$$

How long should n years be? What interest rate should be used? The higher the rate chosen, the less the impact years further out have on price. Ten years is a commonly chosen period, in part because of the declining impact and because projections out that far and beyond become so speculative.

If we continue using our profit projections from Appendix 1, Discounted Income Value over 10 years for those profits looks like this, if we stick with a 15 percent Discount Rate:

Year	Year	Net Profit	Discount Factor	Present Value
1	19X8	$53,699	.869565	$46,694
2	19X9	65,099	.756144	49,224
3	19Y0	78,122	.657516	51,366
4	19Y1	92,968	.571753	53,155
5	19Y2	109,863	.497177	54,621
6	19Y3	129,053	.432328	55,793
7	19Y4	150,819	.375937	56,698
8	19Y5	175,471	.326902	57,362
9	19Y6	203,354	.284262	57,806
10	19Y7	234,852	.247185	58,052
Total Discounted Income Value:				$540,771

Again, different projections will yield a different value. Note, too, the interest rate can also be varied, if one is bold enough to project future market rates and relate them to one's own requirements. (That method is sometimes called "Cyclical Present Value.")

One might ask, "Is it reasonable to cut off valuation after an arbitrary period like 10 years?" Probably not, but the adjustment to remedy the shortcoming will soon be encountered as one of the Combination Methods.

COMBINATION METHODS

Just as Financial Statements describing a business include both an Income Statement and a Balance Sheet, it makes sense that often the most accurate valuation method combines features of both.

The fundamental concept of Combination Methods is that the assets (net of liabilities) have a residual, stand-alone worth, to which is added the Stream-of-Income worth from the operations of the business.

While one alternative for valuation under this concept is simply to match up a favored Asset-Based Value with a similarly favored Stream-of-Income-Based Value, there is more to Combinations than that.

For those wondering why the other two method types have been introduced as valid in their own right if they each tell only half the story, please refer to the very beginning of this chapter.

Excess Income Plus Assets

Excess Income Plus Assets offers simplistic calculations under a sophisticated theory of value. It assumes a company should earn some normal rate of return. Once again, from the buyer's standpoint, that "budgeted" rate should equal the minimum acceptable return. We'll stick with 15 percent.

If that normal rate is applied to equity, it will yield a profit the business should earn. If the business is earning more, it is worth a premium over stated equity; if less, a discount. How much premium or discount? Why, the capitalized value of the profit differential!

The formula reads:

$$E + \frac{(e - (S)(i))}{i}$$

where:

E = current equity

e = earnings

S = starting equity

i = normal rate of return

Taking the latest figures for Sample, 19X7, we find the normal rate of return $[(S)(i)]$ as:

$$(\$241,089)(15\%) = \$36,163.$$

Actual earnings were more, so the excess $[e - (S)(i)]$ is:

$$\$56,671 - 36,163 = \$20,508.$$

The price under this method would then be:

$$297,760 + \frac{20,508}{.15} = \$434,480.$$

Note, if the 7-year average figures were used, the result would be a *discount* from current equity:

$$\text{Average Equity} = \$206,157$$
$$\text{Average Profit} = \$22,358$$

Then:

$$297,760 + \frac{22,358 - (206,157))(.15)}{.15} = \$240,656.$$

Note that we use *current* equity as the base, since that equals the actual Net Assets we would be buying, *but* the differential is based on the averages, since we're trying to get a panoramic view of the business's earning abilities.

This method need not deal only with the past. Projections can be plugged in as easily as historical figures.

The principal criticism of this method is its strength—simplicity. It shortcuts to the question of whether this is a company performing above, below or at the norm, but it's still a shortcut. It addresses inadequately the time value of money, dealing with only a single profit number.

Total Present Value

When we looked at Discounted Income Value, we raised several criticisms. Total Present Value overcomes many of those criticisms. It not only considers projected profits for a discrete time period, but it also includes a value for the net assets the business is projected to own at the end of the time period. For all practical purposes, one is calculating a total investment return, as if the income would be obtained during the period of ownership of the investment, with a cash-out, presumably by sale of the assets and payoff of the liabilities, at the end of the period. Before looking at an example, let's go back to basics for a moment.

The accretion to Net Asset Value will come from profits, assuming no additional investment is made in the company after the initial purchase. In other words, Net Asset Growth must be self-generating, or it will be self-destructing. Yes, the company may borrow to fund asset acquisition, but that's net growth of zero until the loan is paid down. And those loan payments must come from internally generated funds.

If loan payments are roughly equivalent to depreciation, the company will have no growth in Net Assets, except to the extent profits exceed loan payments. If new assets are not bought on credit, then Net Asset Growth will actually be negative as depreciation reduces the asset balances, unless operating profits flowing into retained earnings are high enough to offset depreciation. The issue then becomes "Is the book depreciation an accurate depiction of real depreciation (that is, declination in economic value of the assets)?"

If it is accurate, then, for the purposes of finding Total Present Value, we should use the current Net Asset Value. The reason? Because the future changes that will be wrought in net assets will be produced by depreciation and profits. Those depreciation and profit figures are going to be included in the Present Value of the Income Stream. If they are also considered in the asset change, they will effectively be double counted! So we use the current Net Asset number.

However, if the depreciation is not expected to be a reflection of real change in Asset Value, then the current Net Asset Value has to be adjusted to reflect expected net Market Value at the end of the period.

In our Discounted Income Value we had calculated a 10-year income present value of $540,771. The Net Asset Value at the end of 19X7 on Sample's Books is $297,760 (Book Value) while Adjusted Book Value equalled $391,844. We prefer to have a Market-Value orientation, so we prefer Adjusted Book Value. But Adjusted Book Value has to be readjusted, because one of the original adjustments, the patent, was already valued based on its future income contribution. We can't allow double counting here either.

So, to modify, we reverse out the adjustment to patent value, reducing Adjusted Book Value by $15,000 to $376,844.

On the depreciation versus debt service issue, Sample's figures show depreciation is exceeding loan payments by about $15,000 per year. An analysis further shows the depreciation on real estate about equals the corresponding mortgage principal payments. Thus, the $15,000 excess relates entirely to assets that are declining in value in real economic terms.

Moreover, with a 10-year time frame, we can be confident the total depreciation over that time period will be a real reflection of market economics zeroing out the value of those wasting assets. If a short time period is used the method of depreciation may produce distortion.

Back, though, to the real estate, which is performing in value at variance to its book depreciation. In fact, the real estate is expected to appreciate at 3 percent per year. Since the real estate's fair market value is roughly equal to a quarter of all the assets, that translates to an off-P & L increment of:

$$\frac{3\%}{4} = .75\% \text{ additional growth in assets}$$

To get a Total Present Value, we combine the Discounted Income Value and Adjusted Book Value. If applicable, we modify the latter for the

Market Value growth (or decline) not appearing in the financial statements. Then we find the present value of those assets at the point they're projected to be sold at the end of the buyer's estimated ownership period.

So to get a Total Present Value:

$$DIV \ + \frac{ABVm}{(1 + i)^n}$$

where:

> DIV = Discounted Income Value (see formula in that earlier segment of the chapter)
> ABVm = Adjusted Book Value (possibly modified)
> i = Discount Rate
> n = Time Period

Plugging in the figure we have already developed for Sample, we arrive at a Total Present Value of:

$$540,771 \ + \frac{(1.0075)^{10}(376,844)}{(1.15)^{10}}$$

$$= 540,771 \ + \frac{406,081}{4.046}$$

$$= \$641,148$$

Some may argue that the value of the assets in the business in 10 years certainly will be much greater than the value of assets on hand today, so that there must be some logical flaw in the method. Not so!

The Stream of Income is presumed to be income to the investor, meaning the investor takes it out of the business. True, most investors will leave money in the business for growth, implicitly deciding it's the superior investment opportunity for those funds. Those implicit decisions represent a use of future investment money and it means *additional* investment in the business over *today's* purchase price! We're just looking for a price *today*, and what we care about is the income it will provide and the residual value we can cash in at the chosen time in the future. After all, the smartest investor will *explicitly* decide, at each opportunity for reinvestment, if the business then represents the superior investment choice. If it does not, he or she will hold the money for the better opportunity. The smart investor recognizes it makes no sense increasing the cost of capital by raising capital's opportunity cost component if it can be avoided.

For those who insist they will or must reinvest (perhaps for the psychic

reason of maintaining control over the funds—a form of liquidity preference) the analysis can be modified to:

Find the present value of the stream of reinvestment, which will be an
aggregate subtraction;

Adjust the projections of income if the reinvestments will produce
larger profits;

Project a presumably higher cash-out value for the end of the time
period.

MARKETPLACE METHODS

The whole point of all of the methods is to find out what value makes sense.
Value is a function of the marketplace. But all the methods we've examined
so far may be disputed as focusing too narrowly on the internals of the
company. Marketplace Methods seek to allay such objections by concen-
trating on the external environment, giving an evaluation of the company
by properly pegging its place among the priorities of the market.

Prior Sales

The Prior Sales Method is applicable if the Company has sold shares or if
shares have changed hands among stockholders. Those sales are presump-
tively an indication of market value, as they undoubtedly involved a willing
seller and a willing buyer.

However, if there have been no sales "recently" they may not be a good
indicator. Sales more than a year ago, or prior to a major event or prior to
the release of significant new information are not going to be sufficiently
recent.

Similarly, if the transactions are not "open market" transactions, they
likely have little current meaning. For example, in sales of stock made
under an incentive stock option program the price merely presents a floor
on value, as the employee-buyer would not buy unless the option price was
perceived as below market. Another example would be a company buyback
of stock from an employee under an employment termination provision.

Yet another would be a redemption under a long-term redemption
agreement, where the company was committed to buy back a certain
number of shares each year at a set price. At the time the agreement was
reached, the redemption price probably was a Fair Market Value, but
several years later it's likely to be obsolete.

The exception to such situations will exist if the price is explicitly based on the then-perceived market price, even though the transaction will not occur at that price. For example, if employees are allowed to purchase stock at 10 percent below market value, to reflate employee price to market, divide it by 0.9.

If open market sales data are available, the appropriate company value is easily determined:

$$(\text{Shares Outstanding})\,(\text{Transaction Price per Share})$$

Assume Sample has 100,000 shares outstanding, and the last transaction was for 1000 shares at a price for the lot of $5,000. The value works out to:

$$(100,000)\,(\$5,000/1000) = \$500,000.$$

Where regular sales are occurring or investment houses are making a market in the stock or it's exchange-traded, prices are generally well maintained and easily ascertainable. But in thinly traded, sporadically traded, or even rarely traded issues, pricing may be discontinuous and erratic. Sales occurring near in time may still be quite disparate in price. Disparities are especially likely where transactions are not widely reported or where information is not quickly disseminated. Under those conditions, the numbers must be suspect, but they are useful in providing a range of possible values.

Comparison Values

Every company has its unique characteristics. Nonetheless, there are similarities among different companies, which become more pronounced as qualities like industry, location, staff size, and company age converge. Comparison Values depend on a known price for at least one comparable company. From that "known" one or more financial characteristics of the target are extrapolated to a price for the target.

The most common Comparison Value will use the PE ratios for publicly traded companies in the same industry as the target and then apply it to the earnings of the target. Other comparisons may be based on revenues, total assets, net worth, particular assets (mineral reserves, real estate for example) or particular statistics (such as number of retail outlets for a specialty retailer).

For example, if the average PE for companies in Sample's industry is 8.0 times the most recent 12 months' after-tax earnings, the comparable value for Sample would be:

$$(8.0)(\$56,671) = \$453,368$$

Comparison Values based on figures other than profits are especially useful when a company has a history of losses or is otherwise difficult to nail down. They also are a good safety test of values arrived at using other methods. Two words of warning:

Publicly traded companies are usually well established and well capitalized; and, by definition, investments in them tend to be more liquid. Consequently, a less generous yardstick may be in order for privately held entities. In short, there may not be true comparability.

Secondly, the current market valuation of publicly traded companies is often heavily influenced by the conditions of the market. While these influences are grounded in reality and certainly are "the market," volatility and sudden swings in investor sentiment can create temporary but misleading distortions.

Using an industry average instead of a single company, calculated over time (say the last 12 months average) instead of at a single point in time, tends to defuse the risks.

Market to Book

Although it's really a subset of Comparison Values, Market to Book has a special status because it is so often relied upon. It is a simple ratio; presuming Market Value (price) will always bear a fixed relation to Book Value.

It also has a preferred status among Comparison Values, because it is an Asset-Based Value and is thus likely to be less volatile and less subject to transients than the fragile string of profits or even the less fragile revenues. Those Income Statement figures can be hyped temporarily or distorted by sudden events, from weather to accounting rule changes. Though the Income Statement numbers do fold into the Balance Sheet, one year usually has little impact.

The difficult part is deciding what the proper ratio is. Once again, publicly held companies usually provide the accepted standards, but if superior data is available from another source, use it instead. Taking an average over time usually also adds to the reliability and stability of the method.

If the average price per share for Sample's industry is $63.45, and the Average Book Value per share is $32.30, the ratio is:

$$\$63.45/32.30 = 1.964$$

(Note that in making these calculations, the averages are not weighted by the number of shares, so that the ratio for smaller companies will receive equal treatment. Otherwise the ratio for a larger or more widely held company may unduly skew the analysis.) Therefore, Sample's value would be:

$$(1.964)\,(\$297,760) = \$584,919.$$

All of the criticisms that apply to Book Value may be leveled against this method, but of even greater importance is the question of whether Book Value is really a significant factor in price. Market to Book came to prominence when the economy was far more dominated by production companies. Book Value tends to be less meaningful for the generally labor-intensive service companies, which now predominate.

Revenue Multiplier

A rule-of-thumb valuation method for many small businesses in many industries, especially so-called low-tech industries and smaller retailers, is the Revenue Multiplier method. Although the multiplier is not specifically fixed by any published source, those within the particular industries usually have a feel for the generally accepted one. Many trade associations maintain statistics that include multipliers or data from which they can be derived.

Revenue Multipliers are not arbitrary. Actually, they are a capitalized Stream-of-Income method in disguise. They serve as another shortcut.

Economists will tell us that in a competitive, fractionalized, mature industry, not prone to startling innovation and characterized by relative ease of entry, an equilibrium will be reached. Equilibrium in the real world means competition will cause product (or service) prices, and, hence, profits, to cluster around a norm—a fairly standardized gross margin rate.

Because the costs of servicing the market will also be fairly standardized, overhead among competitors should be fairly comparable. The amount of overhead can similarly be related to sales as a more or less common percentage.

Similarly, capitalization in such situations will also tend to be comparable, as bankers, creditors, and investors will tend to intuitively discern the equilibrium. Their uniform opinions will lead to more standardization in allocating capital to industry participants. In the absence of major changes in the capital markets, those standards will remain in a fairly narrow range.

What about assets? In some industries, the Net Assets may be added to the Revenue Multiplier's price result to arrive at a total price, mirroring the basic concept of a capitalized income stream plus residual value. In Sample's industry, however, the rule-of-thumb ignores assets on the apparent theory that the standard capitalization rate allows for a standard amount of support assets. Not a rocket scientist's approach, it's just a functional shortcut.

In Sample's industry gross profit is normally about 30 percent of revenue and overhead usually runs about 20 percent of revenue. (It doesn't take a lot of effort to see an implied standard profit figure of 10 percent of revenue.) If the assumed standard capitalization rate is 20 percent (a PE of 5), it works out to a multiplier of 0.5 times revenues.

On 19X7's sales, that multiplier would give Sample a value of:

$$(0.5)(\$1,628,947) = \$814,474.$$

This value is quite a bit higher than all the others we have seen. Is there an explanation? Yes, there is.

This method is often used by "mom and pop" operations. They often take benefits out of the business, which show up as expenses, but really are a part of the return to owners. For example, the business may pay them inflated salaries in order to avoid double taxation if the same monies came out as dividends. Expensive autos, insurance, travel and entertainment, and other kinds of expenses may have a personal flavor. A profit-sharing or pension plan may be set up, with benefits heavily skewed toward owners, despite the best efforts of regulators to limit the skewing. Therefore, the real return to owners in the industry is often higher than what is explicitly stated as book profits.

However, Sample's statements are not puffed. If they were, we would have made adjustments to the profit figure much earlier and used an adjusted profit figure for all of the Stream-of-Income methods and Combination methods.

But if Sample hasn't been puffing, does that mean something is wrong with the company? If those standard gross profit and overhead percentages are correct, Sample's performance is lagging. Gross margin averages just 30.7 percent, but four out of the seven years were below the 30 percent standard. More importantly, overhead has averaged a whopping 27.5 percent, a full 7.5 percent over the standard! If a buyer can figure out how to cut overhead, he or she may be able to make this business worth a great deal more. We'll be reviewing this point in some detail at the time of final decision.

Sample's experience points up the risks of oversimplification of the

Revenue Multiplier method, or any similar rule-of-thumb. But it also shows how important questions may be discovered to follow up for meaningful answers. Any buyer and every seller should find out what the industry standards are for business sale pricing, as they will surely be a powerful force in reflecting the market and may lead to vital information.

This prosaic approach is clearly not recommended as a final determinant, because it lacks analytical precision. Yet, it often rears its head and therefore must be dealt with. Consequently, it may map one more boundary on a reasonable price and is likely to provide insight into what your negotiating counterpart may be thinking.

WHICH IS THE BEST METHOD?

It may not be too hard for the reader to sense the author favors Total Present Value. But it's favored because it's likely to provide the best *rational* price. Unfortunately that may differ from the *real* price.

Economists speak of an equilibrium price. That's the same concept as the indifference points we encountered earlier. They mean a price for goods (or businesses) which is just where the transactor can take it or leave it. Below equilibrium price a buyer will buy because he perceives himself better off to have the goods than the money. Above it, he'd rather keep the money. A seller's position is, of course, the mirror image.

Total Present Value is the best method for determining an indifference point. But businesses are not bought and sold in a wholly rational world. Differences in information, resource availability, risk preference, liquidity preference, even the abilities of the parties, and a host of other factors and influences will affect the perception of the parties. As a result, prices that prevail often are not "rational" by an economist's definition, but are what has been chosen by the marketplace, so rational or not, they are *realistic!*

Therefore, in deciding which method to use to value a business, the analyst must operate simultaneously on two potentially converging planes. First, the analyst must decide on an indifference point—a minimum sales price for the seller, a maximum for the buyer. Secondly, the analyst has to decide where, realistically, the market will settle. If the price where the market will settle is outside the indifference point of a party, that party is out of the transaction. If it's outside the indifference points of all the buyers (that is, the seller just prices too high) or the point of the seller (that is, no buyers are making sufficient offers) no transaction will occur.

Divining the market means the analyst has to understand and check whatever method is likely to be employed by the other players. More precisely, the analyst is after the method to be chosen by the player at the margin, who is the person who will make the deal if the analyst does not. Obviously, if the marginal player is on the negative far side of the analyst's indifference point(and some players may just have a different perspective, while others may be plain irrational) it's detrimental to outbid, so the analyst would prefer to let the deal go.

Accordingly, the best method on the market plane is a function of the market itself. Knowing the market, its customs, its players, its idiosyncracies, and its "feel" is the best way to gauge its future. Understand we're talking about the market for a business of this type, not the market to which the business sells, although knowledge about that vending market is usually a major factor influencing the value market for the business.

In many situations the only way to get a good feel may be to run through all, or nearly all, the methods to find a range. Averages, medians, weightings, and other statistical manipulations are worthwhile if they help the analyst. The truth is, there is no method that is always right or wrong, always better or worse, always preferred or disdained. If it works, if it passes the "gut test," it makes sense. There is no magic substitute for business judgment.

One word of caution, though. These methods should not be used to rationalize a senseless price. Once in the market, buyers and sellers are often under many subtle pressures to make a deal happen. Brokers, investment bankers, and others whose income may depend on a successful transaction naturally want to see deals made. Expectations may be raised. Transactors may be inclined to feel like they've failed if they head for the pond and don't come back with a fish. Egos and emotions may be difficult to put aside.

The lure of rationalizing a price is very strong if it looks like others might accept it. Millions of people, sometimes top-flight professionals, have bought stocks at their high, borne along by the psychological grip of the market, rationalizing a price that ultimately proved irrational when the price, with or without the rest of the market, ultimately fell.

Remember, there is no magic substitute for business judgment!

Chapter 4

Value Components

Pricing Influences Beyond
Financial Statements

FLESHING OUT THE FRAMEWORK

The search for rational prices and market values of a business cannot be limited to Financial Statements. After all, businesses are not made up merely of printouts.

But because values are measured in dollars, the analyst must find a way to translate all the attributes not readily reflected in Financial Statements into a component of the financial terms of price and value.

To make the translation, one must first recognize what those attributes are. Some might be called nonfinancial attributes, but others are very definitely financial; they just are not fully shown in the Financial Statements or do not appear at all. Their impact, weight, relevance, potential, probability, and consistency must all be appreciated.

TWO COMPONENT GROUPS

To simplify the process, it is convenient to place each attribute in one of two groups:

Internal Components or
External Components.

Internal Components are those within the control of the company—even though in some cases the company may not recognize or exercise its ability to control them. Asset condition, geographic location, and product mix are three examples. External Components are all the others.

There are some Components that are common to virtually all companies, such as personnel and competition. There are also a few that may be internal for some businesses, while external for others. For example, product pricing freedom (the ability to set revenue prices) is internal for most businesses, although some industries do have price leaders that make great deviation akin to financial suicide. But in other industries regulators set or limit price changes. Regulation is an external force beyond the company's control, though it may be subject to some company influence.

Controllability is important because certainty and stability are valuable to a manager and to a buyer. Conversely, the more susceptible the performance of the business to outside influences, the greater the risk, and the lower the value (all other things being equal, or as the economists say, *ceteris parabus*).

In other words, having established the baseline mathematical value, as we did in the last chapter, the price will go up or down depending on risk. The baseline value, we recall, is a function of the firm's perceived future prospects (regardless of how they may have been explicitly projected or effectively subsumed in the calculations). If the prospects are not realized, any price based on them must, by definition, be in error.

It is conceivable and sometimes true that risks work in favor of the company. It exceeds its prospects, perhaps in spite of itself. The economy unexpectedly booms. Political events suddenly favor its market. For example, terrorism abroad boosts the popularity of domestic vacation spots. A tax law change adds to net.

Shouldn't those windfalls count as much as the chance of a strike, the danger of a lawsuit, the risk of invasive competition, or the probability of a recession? Perhaps they should. In mathematical terms they arguably do in the choice of capitalization rate or revenue multiplier or other gross-up ratio.

But in real terms, something occurs in the dynamics of a business sale that twists the perspective of a transactor, and which must be taken into account in the pricing process: The seller marketing the business determines the shape, scope, and size of the playing field. It is the factors of the business the seller emphasizes that will shape much of the buyer's attitude. The more closely held the business, the more secretive the seller, the more the buyer is forced to depend upon the seller in evaluation. The seller's control is leavened only by what the buyer can investigate independently and the threat of legal action if the seller misrepresents or fraudulently conceals. Even then, time constraints make it hard to get a deep understanding of internal business operations, the dynamics of management and personnel performance, and the details of the company's market relationships, all of which may be the real root explanations of the company's success, mediocrity, or failure.

So, the seller, looking for the best price, is going to put the company's best foot forward. As the old song goes, the seller will "accentuate the positive." A thoughtful and prepared seller will highlight all the good possibilities it is reasonable to imagine. These tend to mark the widest boundaries on the seller's playing field; all proper, all logical, all in the seller's economic interest.

Now the buyer's psychology is curiously self-contradictory. On the one hand, the prudent buyer is being wary and somewhat suspicious. He or she is looking for the chinks in the seller's armor, the skeletons in the closet, the gilt on the lily, and the fly in the ointment. And he badly wants some good arguments to beat the price down during negotiations.

But (and it is a big but) the buyer *wants* to believe the seller. If the buyer is interested in the business, he holds that interest as long as he believes it is the best deal around.

Thus, both parties are likely to be starting their analysis from the rosier side of the spectrum and are therefore each going to need to see their analyses balanced for risk. The buyer must do so to be prudent. The seller must do so to be realistic.

Successful identification of Components and accurate assay of controllability and vulnerability are key for both parties to achieve the best balance. So we shall identify and assess the common Components. It is impossible to develop a truly exhaustive list as each business, each transaction, and each field has its own peculiarities, but this listing is comprehensive for the nearly universal items.

Internal Components

Personnel

Of all the factors one can name, personnel is the most important. Unless competent people, from top executive to part-time laborer, are available to carry out the business plan, the business will suffer. The right people can turn a sow's ear of a company into a silk purse; and the wrong people can (usually much more quickly) have the opposite effect.

Evaluation of personnel is tricky, mostly unscientific, enormously speculative, and indelibly flawed by the fact that by the time the evaluation is complete there will be changes. Changes may be gross in terms of turnover, or more subtle—though painfully real—in terms of shifts in attitude, morale, health, or loyalty.

Before getting into evaluation, let's be sure what it is we are looking for. Generally, we want a workforce that is:

Cohesive: Working well as a team.

Communicative: Hearing and telling fully accurately.

Competent: Able to do their jobs.

Creative: Able to make improvements.

Dependable: Getting the job done on time and on budget.

Ethical: Complying with laws, mores, and ethics.

Honest: Truthful in its dealings and communications.

Self-initiating: Performing with inner motivation.

Loyal: Devoting best business efforts solely to the company.

Obedient: Quickly and carefully carrying out instructions.

Productive: Turning out quality work at a speedy rate.

Stable: Maintaining low turnover and high predictability.

Cost-effective: Exhibiting all those qualities and getting the job done while receiving pay and benefits and generating costs that still permit the company to be competitive and to achieve (high) profitability.

It may sound remarkably like a description of the Boy Scouts of America, but every employer's dream would closely parallel those qualities. How can one measure such human traits? Evaluation is one part discrete, two parts estimable, six parts intuitive, and one part dumb luck.

Let's start with the discrete. Those are the statistics one can gather about the company's roster. The statistical statement should look at both the whole company and the company cross-sections (for example, the sales force). It should yield totals, averages, ranges, and frequencies.

Ideally, it will look not only at the company as it stands today, but also where the company has been. Wouldn't it be interesting, for example, if periods of low profitability correlated to periods of high employee turnover?

A list of statistical measures is included in Appendix 2, with a format to be used to indicate likely correlation to the 13 workforce qualities. Nearly all the statistics can be expressed as per employee or per number of hours worked. Others may indicate percentages, such as contested worker's compensation claims as a percentage of all worker's compensation claims. The analyst must decide what the likely correlations are. We can say, though, that using the one discrete part of statistics allows two parts of estimation (perhaps by correlation) when the analyst's intuition must weigh heavily (six parts) to produce a hopefully (one part dumb luck) accurate picture.

Using those statistics developed from Appendix 2, one can improve estimation, intuition, and maybe even luck by developing templates that may be applied to bring the subjective personnel picture into sharper focus by workforce quality. Some analysts may well perceive more or different desirable qualities, but the technique of statistical itemization and correlation will still apply, even though additional statistics may have to be developed.

Really, the technique is akin to evaluation of sports teams. The baseball team with the best stats has the better chance of winning the pennant. While not a sure bet, it is borne out by the odds and the history of the sport. There is a degree of orderliness in how well people and their organizations perform. Seeing the degree—and how one might influence it—are the analyst's prime task on this point.

The format for a particular template should break down the information by meaningful cross-sections. For example:

Statistic	Total	Management	Support	Sales	Production	Service
Number Employees	87	11	13	19	27	17
Average Age	35	47	28	34	32	38
Average Years Education	14	16	14	15	12	14

Further breakdowns might be warranted in evaluating some groups. Another example:

Statistic	All Production	Supervision	Machining	Finish	Warehouse
Number Employees	27	4	9	11	3
Average Age	32	43	28	31	33
Average Years Education	12	15	11	12	11
Payroll $ (000s)	596	104	207	231	54
Payroll $/ Output*	5.96	1.04	2.07	2.31	0.54

*100,000 units equals last year's output.

Or the statistics might be organized by some other form of cross-section, such as branch sales offices:

Statistic	All Sales-persons	Headquarters	Branch 1	Branch 2	Branch 3
Number Employees	19	7	4	5	3
Average Industry Experience	5	8	4	6	9
Average Company Experience	4	3	4	4	7
# With Restrictive Contract	19	7	4	5	3
Payroll $ (000s)	1140	465	208	261	206
Payroll $/ Employee	60.0	66.4	52.0	52.2	68.7
Sales $ (000s)	20000	7500	3000	5000	4500
Sales $/ Salesperson	1052.6	1071.4	750.0	1000.0	1500.0
Payroll $ % Sales	5.70%	6.20%	6.93%	5.22%	4.58%

Understand this is not meant to indicate that a realistic price can't be determined without going through all of these statistical calculations. Quite the contrary. The point is to provide a method for maximum exploration of the personnel issue. The exploration can be cut back, or even eliminated, as the analyst may choose in light of the company's circumstances, the time and resources available, the importance of personnel to the company's worth, and the inclination of the analyst.

Once through all this statistical data, both raw and manipulated, there are still some personnel questions that do not lend themselves to any sort of measurement, but that may well be important:

1. Who are the leaders in management, especially in each of the key functions?

Administration	Customer Service
Finance/Accounting	Marketing/Sales
Personnel	Planning
Production	Research & Development

Although we might expect to find the titular head of each area the key person, it might not be so. A strong second-in-command, an old hand, a dependable administrative assistant, even an influential secretary may be the "power behind the throne." What we want to know is who is really running the show.

2. Is each of these people desirable? Would each be hired if applying for his or her own job?

3. Will each be a plus (not likely to sabotage the company after a sale, for example) if retained on the staff?

4. Will each stay on, if asked? What incentives might be needed and what will they cost?

5. Will the discharge of any cause severe problems (system breakdown, loss of important customers, morale difficulties, chilling of banking relationships, or other problems)?

6. Are any, if discharged, going to stir up trouble (aiding competitor, filing lawsuit, proselytizing, and so on)?

7. Does the organization chart make sense? Do the positions and the people in them have the optimum relationships for effective functioning?

In all probability, interviews and face-to-face meetings will be necessary to get a good grasp on all these issues. Even then, gut instinct is often the final arbiter.

As the perception of personnel difficulties increases, the value of the business must be affected. The more dependent the business is on fewer individuals, the less its potential value, because of the vulnerability if any are lost. Even when contracts may limit the risk, no guarantees are possible against illness, disability, and death. And people are known to breach agreements.

Rare is the business that can survive without substantial continuity in personnel. Rarer still is the business that retains its full potential value without substantial continuity. Unfortunately no issue is so like quicksilver or so hard to make failsafe. Here is one of these spots where business judgment is crucial.

Customers

Revenues implicitly reflect customer relationships. Looking at a business without an established customer list, such as the typical retailer, limits customer evaluation pretty much to the "feel" of the customer base. The "feel" might be developed from statistics like sales growth, average unit sales, average dollar sales, transactions per time period, and the like.

If it is available, data on the customer base may give insight into marketing strengths and weaknesses. Knowing customers are likely to fit particular profiles may tell a lot about the "quality" of revenues and the likelihood of shrinkage, expansion, and reaction to various marketing efforts.

Where there is a customer list, the rates of turnover and growth tell much about revenue quality as do ordering frequency and order size. In any case, one should ask: Is there a small group of customers accounting for the bulk of revenue? The more concentrated the revenue sources, the more prone to shocks, price-cutting, and decline.

Is the customer group concentrated in a particular way that exposes it to similar risks? For example, if the customer base is made up mostly of the elderly, the base may literally die out if new elderly are not replacing the old. Neighborhood deterioration or redevelopment may destroy a neighborhood-based business. Sales to a single industry, especially a cyclical one, may mean fortunes are tied to the industry. The more positive the outlook for customers, usually the more positive the outlook for the business. (Not so in some cases: bankruptcy liquidators, consumer finance companies, and repair services may thrive when customers are in difficulty.)

The bare revenue numbers must be fleshed out with real customer and market information before their reliability, sensitivity, and projectability can be assessed and factored into decisions.

Support Relationships

These relationships encompass a business's connections with vendors, creditors, insurors, regulators, and organizations such as unions, which affect business operations and prospects. Even when there is much competition for these relationships with the company, existing relationships have an intrinsic value. They require less time. There's less chance of misunderstanding. Response time is likely to be faster. Favors often accrue to be called in someday.

Human relationships, even when clothed as institutional ones, still carry enormous potential for subtle, complex, and far-reaching impact.

Just like the personnel question, the quality and scope of a company's contacts with the outside world cannot be adequately understood from a review of financial statements alone. While undoubtedly subjective, the fruits of investigation are essential to an understanding of what the business is really worth, and, perhaps of greater importance, how it can operate to retain and enhance its worth. Those issues will be in the forefront of a wise buyer's mind as he sets an offer price or mulls a seller's asking price.

Tangible Assets

We spent much time determining fair market values for different kinds of assets. That inspection was a quantitative one, but there is also a qualitative review, which, like personnel, does not lend itself to dead certainty.

The qualitative questions are:

1.   Is there adequate (or excess) capacity?

While this is a question most often thought of with regard to production machinery, it does not end there. Is there adequate data-processing equipment? Is there enough office space? How about warehouse space? Can the phone system handle the load? In short, every major system has to be looked at, not only in terms of what it now handles, but in terms of handling the projected activity. As we've seen, the projections are the key to business price.

If the system will be a constraint, preventing achievement of projections, some adjustment will have to be made. Either projections will have to be reduced, or the cost to upgrade or replace the system will have to be figured into the analysis.

2.   What's the physical condition of these assets?

Maintenance and repair records are particularly useful to see both costs and reliability. Poor condition may indicate morale, cash flow, or other problems. Or it may be a signal to pay particular attention to inventory to be sure damaged and obsolete goods are not being carried at full value. Somebody has to *see* the facilities and the equipment. If the condition is poor, it will take money and time to bring them up to snuff.

3.   Are the systems well organized and compatible?

Particularly, are production systems well integrated? Are data-processing systems fully compatible? Those in the forefront of technology will also want to make sure communications, information systems, and computerized production/handling equipment can communicate with one another.

Organization also refers to documentation, so responsibilities may be handed off to others; and adjustments, such as programming changes, can be made without stress. Repair and maintenance records fit into this part of the review process, too. A company found skipping preventive maintenance may be inadvertently signaling cash is tight.

4. How old are the assets?

The real question here is "How long will these assets remain servicable?" Assets prone to rapid obsolescence may be subject to downward revaluation. Value may also be diminished because of greater difficulty in obtaining replacement parts for older assets.

5. Are the assets properly titled?

Legal ownership should be clearly and inviolably established. It is obviously foolish to pay for assets that can't be bought. Mistakes most often arise over leased assets or those purchased on installment contracts. Also verify there are no liens on the assets, or make provisions for release of the liens as part of the transaction. Alternatively, the buyer may be granted a credit for taking responsibility for the payoff of the lien.

Clouded ownership will certainly reduce the price. The more crucial the asset the greater the potential reduction. Title is one of the areas a prudent seller will get squared away before putting the business on the market. Many a deal has broken down over the surprise of clouded title on one asset or another. This is not without good reason, for a buyer has a right to be skeptical when such a fundamental and controllable issue is discovered in disarray.

6. Are the assets secure; that is, safe from theft, vandalism, and other hazards?

Risk from those kinds of hazards has the same impact on price as any other kind of risk. A business located in a high crime area is going to carry a lesser value, again all other things being equal.

7. Are the assets themselves hazardous?

Are they dangerous to operate? Do they pose an environmental risk? Are facilities unsafe for customers, vendors, and other visitors, as well as workers? Are any assets not in compliance with laws, regulations, or ordinances? If any are uninsurable, that may be a sure sign of high risk.

Once regarded as of minor importance, these issues now are fraught with potentially catastrophic financial risks, assuming one can be cold-hearted enough to ignore moral implications and foolish enough to ignore morale implications.

Intangible Assets

Except for the questions relating to physical qualities, the same questions apply to intangibles as to tangibles. Additionally, one should ask: Have all the intangibles been recognized? Even as simple a matter as retaining the seller's phone number may be critical to justifying a price.

Are all registrations and legal rights properly on record? Have trade-marks, copyrights, and patents been properly maintained and vigorously protected? Are all licenses, both commercial and regulatory, transferable? Can they be transferred without significant cost?

Might technology eviscerate the value, especially of patents, secret formulas, and confidential processes? Similarly, could shifts in public attitudes downgrade the value of trademarks or advertisement copyrights? For example, a restaurant chain trademark featuring a cozy couple might actually be a detriment if they're both holding lit cigarettes.

Could regulatory changes hurt the value of government-granted per-mits? Such devaluation occurred in the trucking industry when it was deregulated.

Are secrets indeed secret and safeguarded? That question does not ask merely about the risk the secret has leaked out or might soon. It also inquires about the uniqueness. Have others stumbled on the same discov-eries or might they, in fact, be fairly common, in one form or another, in the trade? Likewise, do they really have any value? And, once again, are all the legal protections, often in contract form on this score, in place?

As a franchisee or licensee, is there a risk the franchisor or licensor will encounter difficulty and fail to live up to its promises? Might it go bankrupt or attempt to renege on promises? In other words, how solid is the third party implicitly relied upon if the franchise or license is given any material value. Similarly, can the lessor be relied upon in a lease, whether for real estate or equipment?

Intangibles often get short shrift in transactions involving small, closely held businesses. They deserve more scrutiny, especially by sellers, who may find justification for a higher price.

Liabilities

Presumably the Balance Sheet accurately reflects all the liabilities realized as of the books-closing date. But what about those not yet realized?

True, CPA-prepared statements are supposed to footnote "contingent liabilities," but such items must have been formalized in some sense to appear. For instance, an affiliate's debt must have been guaranteed, or the company's attorney has certified a lawsuit may be filed against the company.

The bigger dangers are the ones not yet formalized. The product line afflicted with defects eventually must be recalled. The environmental and safety hazards to and generated by assets earlier alluded to must be dealt with. The tax audit yet to occur may be costly. The reratings for employee insurance, unemployment taxes, and worker's compensation not yet declared will increase expenses. The municipal assessment still unannounced raises overhead.

One can always imagine enough demons out there to rationalize the killing of any deal and the denigration of any price. The trick is to consider real evidence to decide what is likely to matter. The easy example is a material deduction in the tax return not likely to be accepted if audited by the IRS. The tougher example is the identification of hazardous waste material generated in the production process.

Then, once the real potential liabilities are identified, the bigger trick is to see if they might be overcome. Generally, there are three ways to handle the bigger trick:

1. Eliminate (or at least limit) the risk. For example, replace the dangerous machinery.
2. Shift the risk. Get an indemnity agreement from a third party, such as the manufacturer of the machinery.
3. Insure the risk.

The associated costs and risks then may be included in the value calculations. More on the methodology for inclusion in the next chapter.

Quality of Earnings

One of the most important considerations in analyzing the financial statements of a company is the so-called "Quality of Earnings." Because of accounting conventions, it is altogether possible for a business to regularly report profits, while heading straight for bankruptcy. More often, profits are pumped up, deliberately or accidentally, in the sense that the profits are not reflected in a real increase in assets. (Of course, if profits are distributed to owners in the form of cash or other company assets, then the assets retained in the business will be correspondingly less.) Businesses with Net Assets increasing more slowly in real economic terms than are shown in the Financial Statements are said to have a poor quality of earnings.

Alternatively, it is also possible for the reverse situation to occur; that is, the business is in fact building wealth at a faster rate than is reflected in stated earnings. Under those conditions, the business is said to have a good or excellent quality of earnings. Earnings that are a realistic statement of profitability are also deemed to be good in quality.

How might these differences occur? Several of the most common accounting vagaries that can lead to divergence between stated and real earnings are:

1. Depreciation differs from the true change in value of the assets being depreciated. Depreciation sometimes overstates earnings, sometimes understates them.

2. Appreciation in assets is often not booked until realized by sale or other disposition of the asset. The failure of the appreciation to appear on the Financial Statements will understate earnings.

3. Retention of Bad Debts as Accounts Receivable will overstate earnings.

4. Retention of worthless or devalued inventory at its original cost will also overstate earnings.

5. Inventories that fluctuate in value (raw materials, for example) can cut both ways. The greater the percentage of assets made up of such inventories, the more questionable the true economic worth and performance.

6. Inventory accounting also has a marked potential to misstate earnings, especially where the elements of cost going into inventory have experienced major change in levels through inflation or other factors. Restating earnings on one or more additional inventory methods is an especially good way to evaluate the impact and the quality of the earnings, though it may be difficult for a buyer to get adequate information to do so with precision. From the seller's standpoint, it may make sense to consider changing inventory valuation methods, if the embedded method is going to make a sale more difficult or less rewarding.

7. Failure to accrue obligations overstates earnings. Some of the commonly unaccrued but real obligations are such items as employee vacation

pay, warranty repairs, product liability claims, payroll insurance adjustments (worker's compensation insurance is often backcharged after audit at the end of each policy period), promotional costs (the cost of servicing or fulfilling promotional promises, such as an airline's frequent flyer obligations), and the infamous unfunded pension liability.

8. Foreign exchange considerations can have a marked effect on the profits of companies doing a material amount of overseas business. The variations from foreign exchange can cut both ways, but the effects are made more complicated by the timing of repatriation (conversion to home currency) of the earnings.

9. Capitalized expenses, such as Research and Development costs, will tend to overstate earnings; although if the outcome is the development of an income-producing asset with worth, capitalization may prove to be the correct decision in the long run.

10. In closely held businesses, true profitability may be understated by larger payouts in the forms of excessive salary, bonuses, interest payments, auto expenses, travel, and other personally flavored items, all of which the owner has the tax incentive to treat as other than profits during normal operations. These characterizations can catch up with an owner at the point of sale, as buyers will often be rightfully skeptical of claims of profits far above those appearing in the Profit & Loss Statement. Nonetheless, such claims often turn out to be bona fide and bear investigating.

The more debatable the accounting practices and the heavier the concentration of equity in suspect assets, the lower the quality of earnings. Sellers must be prepared to defend their accounting practices. Buyers must be on the lookout for questionable statements, and must be able to assess the risk that the statements may be signaling something different about a company's prospects and worth than what they may appear to be or are claimed to be signaling at first blush.

It is because of these concerns that Cash Flow Statements (sometimes called Statements of Sources and Uses, Funds Flow Statements, and Working Capital Statements) have become of greater interest to analysts, accountants, and managers in recent years. The operative theory behind their popularity seems to be that cash is the ultimate asset. If there is adequate cash on hand, and if cash is increasing, the business is safe.

Those views deserve some credence. Business people cannot ignore cash flow and the constraints and opportunities cash availability affects. But cash is not the Holy Grail, and Cash Flow Statements are not the secret to a company's past or future. They are an element, and they deserve attention.

Though Quality of Earnings deals with numerical values, it is a component requiring intensive subjective scrutiny. If earnings are materially misleading in terms of real return, they should be restated in the course of the analyst's preparations, and the results rolled into the rest of the calculations, especially those for projections and in determining a fair value for the assets to be acquired in the course of a transaction.

One special word of caution here: If the statements are found to be out-of-whack by a substantial amount, that's fair warning to a buyer of potential danger that transcends mere pricing issues. It may be signaling that the business is built on a foundation of sand, or even more seriously that the seller is not on the level. Fraud is not unknown. If that kind of issue rears its head, the prudent buyer will only go forward if the issue can be proven to have been raised in error. No amount of risk adjustment or price revision is going to compensate for those kinds of problems.

Tax Attributes

With frequent changes in the federal tax system, often with repercussions on state, local, and international taxation, this is a topic in flux. Depending on the nature of the business and the type of deal being struck, the tax attributes of the seller may or may not enter into the buyer's equation, other than as background information.

Still, where carryforwards, depreciable bases, unused credits and the like may exist, they ought to be factored into net profits for the relatively short-term in which they normally may apply. However, some commentators may well argue little faith should be placed in these attributes. The key arguments are that they are transient, short-term, and subject to revision, especially given the legislative trend toward denying transferability.

In any event, a deal dependent upon tax benefits or on a particular tax treatment is almost certainly one open to criticism and its object is subject to devaluation. One principal reason for the assertion is the fundamental one that a deal must be grounded in solid economics. Tax advantages should be icing on the cake, not the batter.

The second reason is controllability. Tax advantages granted by government may be just as easily rescinded by government. Each governmental decree is beyond the control of the company, the buyer or the seller.

Research and Development

It is remarkable how the exchange-traded securities of many companies are suddenly inflated by the announcement of some product introduction or research development. Yet in private sales, these "birds in the bush" usually receive far less attention than a single "bird in hand."

Indeed, this is an area worth exploring. The quality of research and development, if it exists at all in the business, may tell much about the ability of the company to respond to or even incite change in the marketplace. In that sense, R&D is another possible index of revenue quality.

What is in the pipeline may also influence upon which end of the price range one wants to land. However, prudence dictates that only very rarely will the gleam in an inventor's eye justify dollars not elsewhere supportable. No one wants to pass up the next Xerox, Apple, or Genentech; but the number of failures far exceeds the number of successes—even the number of breakevens plus successes. Just ask any seasoned venture capitalist.

External Components

The world in which a business exists can have all sorts of wondrous and surprising impacts on the business—some good, some bad. Trying to predict the future of the world is an impossible exercise. But it is possible to consider several general categories of events and conceive probable impacts for which the business ought to be prepared. If one or more of these exogenous influences is ultimately brought to bear, how it will affect the prospects and performance must ultimately be a consideration in the fixing of a value and a price.

Seeking objective mathematical assurance wherever it may be found, it is worth noting this is another area where statistical methods like correlation may be outstandingly useful. Many of the possible outside influences are facets of the economy that are mirrored in the many published statistics, and thus available for analysis.

For example, assume Sample Company's history shows its gross margin tends to decline as inflation increases. Is that a logical relationship or a mere coincidence? In fact it does make sense, because Sample is in a highly competitive industry in a geographic market populated with many competitors. Sample consequently has trouble raising prices. Costs go up more rapidly than product prices.

Secondly, is it a quantifiable relationship? Prices have been increased without too much resistance up to 4 percent per year. But every point of inflation above 4 percent erodes gross margin by $2/3$ percent. On the other hand, an inflation rate below 4 percent does not increase gross margin: because in those circumstances Sample has been forced to hold down price increases in line with the economy, or has used the opportunity to run promotions that effectively nullify the excess.

Such information is useful in simulating possible outcomes using different inflation projections. It also would imply a lower business price if it looks like inflation is going to exceed 4 percent for an extended period.

Thirdly, one must ask if the relationship should continue to hold. Has the business been insufficiently aggressive in raising prices or in justifying the price increases? Is it too lax in response to vendor increases in prices? Is the relationship true across the whole product line or might a different sales mix ameliorate the problem? If the way is clear to overcome this impediment, a higher price for the business may be reasonable. Or, better yet from the buyer's viewpoint, the buyer may justify the lower price based on the disadvantageous correlation yet earn a higher rate of return by overcoming the problem.

What are the general categories that ought to be considered?

Economy

The more a business's performance tends to fluctuate with the economy, the less confidence one can have in it, because of the implication that it is not a company in control of its own destiny. More frightening is the business whose fluctuations, particularly on the downside, are more exaggerated than the economy it follows.

Mostly all businesses are affected to one degree or another by the economy, but more specificity is required to achieve a meaningful understanding of the relationship.

Gross National Product (GNP)

When people talk about the economy, they first address the measure of growth or recession, the GNP. For businesses whose market is confined to a community or a region, Gross Metropolitan, State, or Regional Product—or other similar figures—are often available.

Businesses following cyclical patterns are at least fairly predictable, even though some of the predictability may be negative. Such a finding surely means projections are due for cross-checking.

Another telling point is the comparison of growth rates, company to GNP. A company may still be growing, but if growth is slower than the applicable economic measure, it may be a sign of trouble ahead.

Inflation

Another prominent economic measure, the inflation rate is often mirrored in cost ratios rather than in sales. The refinement, sometimes the key to a clear picture, is choosing the correct inflation index. There are regional indices as well as a national number. Then there are choices among the Consumer Price Index, the Wholesale Price Index, the Commodity Price Index, and others.

There are also industry indices. It is not unusual to find some indices relate to one aspect of the business, while others apply elsewhere. Commodity Prices may be a good measure for cost of goods sold, while Personal Income may relate to labor costs. Whether or not one should seek such specificity is a function of the materiality of the costs or revenues being evaluated.

Interest Rates

The more capital intensive the business, the greater the impact interest rates are likely to have. Similarly, if the business's customers are sensitive to interest rates, there again may be a strong, though technically indirect, impact on prospects.

What is positive from a valuation standpoint is a business where changes in interest rates have little effect, at least when swinging between historically normal levels.

International

With globalization of economies continuing apace, more and more companies are finding an inescapable connection with nondomestic activity. Specific subinformation on foreign economies is often hard to get and frequently tends to be less than reliable. The domestic "contact" numbers—such as balance of trade, balance of payments, exchange rates, and port activity—may often be the most readily available and the most relevant. Beyond that, analysis proceeds as it does with the comparable domestic figures.

Industry Activity

Investigation of this category often yields bonus information. The bonus information comes as a preview of competition and in seeing the strengths and vulnerabilities of the industry versus the economy at large. Both are desirable background.

Basically, the relationship of the industry's activity level to the company's activity is a micro approach to economic questions. Activity refers to the economic standard being evaluated, such as GNP, inflation, employment growth, wage rates, return on assets, or whatever. Lagging performance suggests a lower price, while superior performance may mean an increase. These measures deserve special attention in utilizing an industry-based pricing method, such as revenue multipliers.

If the firm's customers are concentrated in one industry, it also makes sense to look at the prospects for the customer industry. They may well foreshadow the target's prospects. Industry statistics, especially if they're to be broken down to the narrowest definition of the industry, may be better obtained from trade associations than government sources.

Other Economic Factors

Depending on the level of economic sophistication, one can explore any number of details to see if there is a subtext indicator or group of indicators for performance: housing starts, stock market data, rail traffic, steel production, average workweek, new business formations, manufacturing capacity, electricity output. There's no shortage of possibilities.

Remember, though, the goal is to discover if the business is going to be sensitive to an externality that may underlie or undermine projections. The goal is not a statistical exercise. Consequently, a rational link to a chosen measure must exist. Meaningless coincidence can occur. Relying on it will ultimately prove mistaken.

Technology

We touched earlier on the technology risk as it relates to patents and other intangibles. But technological risk is not limited to obsoleting a product or process.

Technology may also affect the level of competition. For example, the advent of the home videocassette recorder and the introduction of music videos suddenly created a new medium of competition for the vinyl record industry.

Technology can additionally affect the level of demand. The development of desktop publishing bit off a chunk of the market for graphics firms.

Or technology can wipe out the value of an inventory and the market it was designed to serve. The classic example of the auto industry destroying the buggy whip industry comes quickly to mind.

Technology's effects may be manifested in the cost profile, as substantial new investment in equipment may become essential to remain competitive. The steel industry knows this phenomenom all too well.

So the questions to ask about technology are:

How does the company compare in technological sophistication to the industry? If the target does not look too strong it indicates a lower price, especially if large expenditures will be required to catch up.

How frequent are significant technological changes in the industry? The more frequent the changes the greater the risk.

How prone to technological risk is the company? In other words, how likely is it a technological change could disrupt a material part, or all, of the outfit's sales, operating, or profit strategy? The more dependent the company is on a single product, a narrow market, a limited margin, or other fragile element, the more exposed it is to this kind of risk, and the more vulnerable its price to reduction. This is an area where parties are often complacent if there have not been changes in a long time. It does not mean there might not be changes in the future. Several generations of blacksmiths took demand for their skills as a given, until one day the horseless carriage made its appearance.

Competition

Except for a few public utilities, every business has its competitors; and even with the utilities, one may substitute oil heat for gas heat, or gas for electric. The central issue of competition is not its existence, but its stability. If it is changing, are the changes likely to be significant enough to materially affect revenues, either through price-cutting or by threatening unit sales?

Assessment of competition is always difficult and subjective. The toughest part is predicting new entries, whether in the form of startups, diversifications, geographical expansions (including imports), or indirect competition in the form of substitutes competing in a new marketplace.

In truth it is nearly as difficult to gauge the vigor and potential impact of existing competitors. The frequency and intensity of price wars, the extent of advertising, the number of salespersons on the road, and other pieces of intelligence should help to close in on an accurate judgment.

Competition is always sort of a loose cannon on the business deck, and one that might be most feared because it is usually the only uncontrollable element intentionally out to do harm to the firm. On the other hand, the known enemy is usually less dangerous than the unknown. Recognizing the constant of competition limits its importance in the business pricing equation, unless high potential for significant change in the scope of competition is at hand.

Regulation

If competition is a loose cannon, many might argue the plethora of government authorities, from municipalities to federal agencies, equals a loose grenade minus its pin. While the assessment of this or that regulation may be of transient importance, the core issue is the *extent* of regulation. The greater the extent of regulatory control over operational decisions, most importantly rate or revenue regulation, the more vulnerable the company is to damage, and the riskier full valuation becomes.

Social Tastes and Social Risks

Any business whose sales and profits are temporary will have a finite value determinable to the end of the sales period. One does not want to pay a long-term value for a fad.

If sales are vulnerable to a shift in social tastes, and the shift will not favor some other equally profitable revenue source for the company, price must suffer.

Similarly, if the business risks public or consumer wrath, the extent of the risk must be considered in a regulatory context. Environmental, political, ethnic, and moral stances or factors laden with the chance of controversy are inherently risky. Keep in mind, though, that a change in ownership may be just the ticket to defuse the controversy. Sometimes, too, controversy may be a plus if it generates useful publicity without overbearing cost.

Political Events

A business vulnerable to political developments is at risk. In point of fact, every business is vulnerable to political events, the extreme example being global war. The issue here is abnormal political risk.

For example, a business with material sales and profits dependent on a controversial government project, or obtained through political patronage, are suspect. Businesses with a high percentage of international sales may also be questioned, the more so if the sales are concentrated in areas of unrest.

Unlike social taste, political risks are not limited to the sales equation, especially in the international arena. Vital supplies or materials might become unobtainable or prohibitively expensive. Deliveries may be interdicted in either or both directions. Funds may be impounded preventing payment, not to mention the ever-present susceptibility of currency exchange rates to political turmoil.

Yet, one does not want to overestimate the importance of a momentary disruption without lasting meaning. It is similarly critical to avoid overreacting to political issues within the range of the normal "noise level."

Resource Stability

Any business dependent for resources upon one outsider or a narrow group also has a kind of vulnerability. The premier example is the manufacturer depending upon a parts supplier for a key part, where the patent on the part is tightly controlled by the supplier.

One risk is the danger of failure of the supplier. A more frequently encountered downside experience is rising supplier prices without the ability to raise output prices at the same rate. The risk of supply interruption, as from a strike, should not be a factor unless the interruptions are likely to occur with such frequency that earnings prospects are regularly or permanently affected.

Also worthy of mention is the business whose value is predicated on accelerating growth. If the supplier's capacity proves to be a constraint, slower growth may be inevitable with concommitant results for value.

If alternative sources might be developed, or technology might eliminate the risk, or some other fortuitous circumstance limits instability to a normal level (that is, a level comparable to standard business risks) value will probably not require adjustment.

When mere materials are involved, there is a good possibility backups eventually can be found. Some other types of resources may be literally irreplaceable to the point survival may be threatened or loss would be permanently crippling. The best example is the successful franchisee, whose success is built on the franchise relationship. Loss of the franchise or failure of the franchisor likely means curtains for the franchisee.

Labor Stability

While arguably just a subset of personnel, labor stability deserves distinct mention because the issue goes beyond the internal questions already addressed. If an adequate and competent labor pool is not available at acceptable cost, business value is suspect; and the suspicion increases if growth could be squelched by labor shortage. The more labor intensive the company, the larger these concerns must loom.

Labor markets and workforce quality are tough to judge and often are in a state of some evolution. So the personnel statistics templates may be used to some extent in contemplating labor externals.

Another aspect is the possibility unionization may affect value. Most business owners are inclined to think a unionized company is riskier than a nonunion shop. While the conventional wisdom holds true more often than not, this labor issue is not so simple. One cannot throw a minus sign in somewhere simply because some of the employees are carrying union cards.

Statistics propounded by some unions show unionization is a sign of, if not a promoter of, labor stability in some industries. Where the quality of the company-to-union relationship is a good one, the order, uniformity, communication lines, and qualification standards that unionization and collective bargaining may bring are a plus. If the bulk of competition has also been organized, union presence may well be a nonissue.

COMPONENTS SUMMARY

The overriding message about these components is to be alert for the variances, exceptions, changes, and quantum-leap shifts portending a permanent, material alteration in prospects, profits, and entity price. Controllability, stability, and predictability support or even add to the baseline price. Unruliness, volatility and uncertainty tend toward subtraction.

Controllability does not mean inevitability. Stability does not mean no growth. Predictability does not mean a simple straight line. The fundamental goal is to be so positioned that the buyer's optimum business plan can be managed to achieve maximum benefit, thereby entitling the seller to the best price. Impediments endanger the interests of both. Solutions aid both.

Chapter 5

Components Assessment to Final Price

Decision Time

AVOIDING ANALYSIS PARALYSIS

Before quantifying the impact on value of all these components, a word about being practical must be inserted.

Risk is a given. Uncertainty is a given. Change is a given. Fallibility is a given

It is always possible to retain the status quo by overemphasizing these givens as too much of a deterrent. Or by striving to cover every base, it is also possible to default to the status quo. By the time every last one of the cited issues can be thoroughly explored, circumstances will change, and sooner or later the seller will lose interest, lose faith in the buyer's credibility as a transactor, or find another deal, So, too, the seller who procrastinates over setting a real price will find buyers looking, and eventually making a deal elsewhere.

Finding the prudent middle ground, developing sharpened senses of the dynamics of a deal, and proceeding with competent business judgment are not abilities easily taught. While experience may be the best teacher, it can also be the most expensive, and, for most business owners and would-be owners, it is hard to come by.

What, then, makes sense?

DEAL APPRECIATION

How much effort should go into component valuation? How much time can be afforded? How strongly should the findings weigh in the final conclusions?

As a general rule, the more significant the potential transaction, the greater the care that must be exercised, the greater the time to be expended, and the greater the weight the findings will carry.

If a buyer is using up all capital, failure will be catastrophic. The same is true if the buyer is an existing business growing by acquisition, and a poor acquisition will ruin the whole enterprise. In a similar vein, if the seller has but one business to sell and is selling the entire business (not just a part) it is an all-or-nothing, do-or-die proposition.

In every deal, all of the components should at least be reviewed. It is best to start the review by prioritizing items according to materiality. The most significant risk should be listed first. In the priority process, some items are likely to be dismissed as unimportant, especially when time is limited or investigative resources are stretched. Near the end of the evaluation process, the list should be reviewed again, with special care given to the lower rated and dismissed items, to be sure nothing critical has been overlooked or erroneously assumed.

The old saw, "Time kills deals," is usually true. If a deal is to be made, the parties must move with deliberate speed. They must each nail down the essential fundamentals, focus on the key issues, consider all the peripheral matters, evaluate all the components, and attend to the exceptional ones.

Then each party must make a decision.

QUANTIFICATION CHOICES

Before making the decision, though, just how can meaningful data about the price-influencing components be translated into the pricing decision?

When all of the basic valuation methods are reconsidered, their input variables are really all one of three types:

Net Asset Values (accounting by offset for liabilities);

Profits (which may be stand-alone, averaged, or projected);

Discount Rate (whether expressed as an interest rate, or as some kind of multiplier).

Therefore, the effect of the components must logically be measured in these terms. In some cases, more than one type will be involved.

Net Asset Values

If the component affects the Balance Sheet, it's pretty easy to envision the impact on value, whether it would show up on the asset side or the liabilities side.

For example, when we adjusted the Balance Sheet to get the Fair Market Value of assets, the real estate's worth was elevated to $150,000. But what if the business is using the building under a special zoning exception, one which will by its terms be forfeit if ownership of the property or the business changes hands? Moreover, once that permissive zoning is lost, the value of the property declines, for the other uses that would then be permitted are not as desirable. In fact, the property value would fall by 20 percent to $120,000 as a result. Therefore, the current Fair Market Value under the present operation is $150,000, but the resale value is something markedly different.

Now, there are four quite noteworthy points about this example:

First, the 20 percent differential, equal to $30,000, is material in a transaction of this size.

Secondly, because it affects a Balance Sheet item, a part of the tangible value, it is very definitely not a transient matter.

Thirdly, and perhaps most momentously, this readjustment illustrates the kind of operational detail that often is not readily apparent from just a review of financial documents or even a wide range of internal documents. Investigation beyond the company is likely to be required (in this case with the zoning authorities and among municipal records) to get a true picture.

Fourthly, it is also the sort of discovery that has ramifications beyond the balance sheet. It is an item that potentially crosses into all three types of input variables, as we shall see.

Profits

The profit a buyer cares about is the future profit. History is important only as prologue, and it may be misleading.

As each of the prioritized risks is examined, one can estimate the likely effect on profits if the risk is realized. The historical prologue, manipulated and massaged though it may be, provides the starting point for considering the impact.

Let's expand on the Sample Company zoning example: Not only does loss of the zoning exception affect the Balance Sheet, but it will hit the

Profit and Loss Statement, too. The expenses involved in moving to a new location will cause the initial damage. The long-term hit is caused by a sales decline due to the greater distance from current customers. The sales decline will eventually be reversed, but it pushes the payoff further out and means lower income in the earlier years, which count the most heavily when present value methods are applied.

The change in location inputs another permanent detriment. The greater distance to both vendors and customers will raise freight costs. Even if these costs could be passed on to customers as higher prices or add-on charges, they still detract from the company's competitive position. And we already know Sample Company is in a market with some pretty stiff price resistance, especially if inflation runs above 4 percent.

There are three lessons to be drawn from the extension of the example:

First, the short-term disruptions are not very important, unless they are unusually large, because a temporary blip in profits does not denigrate the fundamental worth of the company. In fact, the reasonable way to treat short-term expenditures is to reduce net assets as if a reserve (for example, estimated relocation expenses) were set up on the books, assuming the issue in question is material enough to merit an adjustment.

Conversely, items with long-term consequences matter very much, because they go to the central point of return on investment.

Lastly, knowledge about these dangers should alert the analyst to consider how the negatives can be countered. Is there a chance the move can be used to *increase* sales by generating extra sales in the new location, while holding on to old customers, perhaps by rechanneling advertising or reworking the marketing budget to make room for some kind of special promotion? Could relocation spur some new supplier relationships, which might offer new terms or prices sufficient to offset the freight differential? Maybe it's time for the company to reconsider the economics of its own delivery fleet?

In short, identifying the problems can serve as a basis for planning to overcome the negatives, and for avoiding downgrading of the bottom line. In these deliberations, absolute precision cannot be assured, but it is not essential. The objective is a conceptual handle on prospects so a range of values can be locked onto.

Discount Rate: Concept

Asset and profit figures are grounded in the Financial Statements. As the statements spring from the operations and circumstances of the business itself, it is not difficult to relate the figures to the known reality of those operations and circumstances, even when making projections into the future.

Discount rate figures are, in contrast, somewhat less controllable and somewhat more tenuous. They are derived from market forces and market alternatives. In times of volatility or instability in the financial markets, a discount rate is an even more debatable pricing coefficient.

The beauty of the discount rate, though, is its ability to summarize a broad range of risks, uncertainties, perils, and concerns into a single mathematical operator. These summarized contingencies may even be unrelated to one another, except for the fact that they all affect the business.

The axiom defining the discount rate operator is:

"Higher risk demands justification of a higher rate of return."

The first corollary to the definition is:

"As the aggregate degree of risk increases, the discount rate must rise to compensate."

The second corollary to the definition is:

"As the aggregate degree of risk decreases, the discount rate may fall in response."

The third corollary to the definition is:

"If the aggregate degree of risk does not materially deviate from the norm, the discount rate should approximate the standard market rate."

Pursuing the zoning exception example, there are several possible outcomes:

One outcome is the buyer successfully applying to the authorities for a permanent zoning waiver or a zoning change. Such an outcome would, by the way, vouchsafe the full $150,000 asset value, minus only the costs of obtaining the preferred outcome.

A second outcome is replication of the seller's special zoning exception, continuing the operation, but subject to the same exclusion at the point of resale by the buyer. The effect on asset value then would be to reduce it to the lower value, as its Fair Market Value to the buyer immediately after the sale would still be only $120,000. However, that's the only change to the business price, as profits will not need to be reduced.

A third potential outcome would be a loss of the zoning, but a splitting of operations, so the offending portion (perhaps the manufacturing activities) might be relocated, leaving the nonoffending portions (such as sales, warehousing, and administration) at the site. Then the property would still have some use and only some of the losses would be incurred.

Assetwise, the property value drops to $120,000. On the profits side, the sales retention, partial moving expense reduction, and freight out savings must be compared with the greater costs of operating two facilities, including otherwise unnecessary intracompany freight.

Or, perhaps, a way can be found to make the operations conform, so the zoning revision will not be so meaningful. The building value will fall, but only the costs of conformance will have to be factored into the calculations. If up-front and one-shot in nature, they'll be treated as a reservation reduction in assets. If ongoing, they'll reduce profit projections.

Lastly, of course, the confirmed worst case, the property becomes unusable and a move is required, with the attendant losses and expenses already detailed.

Note that the assumption a single outcome must occur is itself an analytical risk. The buyer demands some higher reward for all this risk and uncertainty, so the discount rate is the logical place to make the adjustment.

Discount Rate: Practice

All those general statements are helpful and interesting, but how do they get translated into a concrete rate leading to a firm price? Once again we refer to the market.

Most financial managers are familiar with yield curves, of which there are two basic types:

Time-Sensitive Yield Curves

Risk-Sensitive Yield Curves

The Time Sensitive Yield Curve shows how interest rates obtainable on debt securities (bonds, for example) of *comparable risk* will vary by length of maturity. It says, "If risk is held constant, this is how interest rates vary with the time the money will be tied up." Normally, the yield will increase as the time until the maturity date gets longer. A longer wait until maturity means there is increased uncertainty and increased opportunity cost. Longer maturities (beyond the very short run) also run counter to the common liquidity preference of most investors.

Following is a set of data and its graph (Figure 5.1), which demonstrate a Time Sensitive Yield Curve for U.S. Treasury Securities.

The Risk-Sensitive Yield Curve shows how interest rates obtainable on debt securities of *like maturities* will vary by degree of risk. As we've already noted, as the degree of risk rises, the rate rises to compensate for it.

U.S. TREASURY SECURITIES YIELD TO MATURITY

Maturity	Yield Rate (%)
3 mos.	5.85
6 mos.	6.37
1 yr.	6.62
2 yrs.	7.21
3 yrs.	7.47
4 yrs.	7.64
5 yrs.	7.81
10 yrs.	8.23
20 yrs.	8.38
30 yrs.	8.49

Figure 5.1: Time-Sensitive Yield Curve: U.S. Treasury Securities

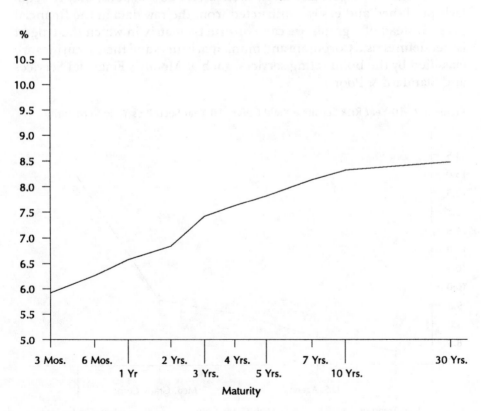

Here's an example of data for 10-year securities, with a graph (Figure 5.2) showing the Risk-Sensitive Yield Curve:

10-YEAR SECURITIES: YIELD TO MATURITY			
Risk Type	Yield Rate (%)	Risk Type	Yield Rate (%)
U.S. Treasury	8.23	Medium Grade Corporate	9.75
U.S. Agency	8.66	Low Grade Corporate	13.00
High Grade Corporate	9.29		

As both curves share a common axis (yield rates) they could be portrayed in combined form as a planar surface on a three-dimensional graph, but that's too difficult to show or read clearly on this two-dimensional page, so the everyday financial world continues to use the two-step process for consideration. No doubt, when holographic "paper" becomes as commonplace as pulp-made paper, a single graph will appear in the financial press, the touchstone for widespread use.

Financial managers also know these aren't abstractions; they're regularly published and easily constructed from the raw data in the financial press. Instead of a graph, we can construct a matrix in which the type of issuer defines risk. Corporate and municipal issuers and their securities are classified by the bond rating services, such as Moody's Financial Services and Standard & Poor's.

Figure 5.2: 10-Year Risk-Sensitive Yield Curve: 10-Year Securities Yield to Maturity

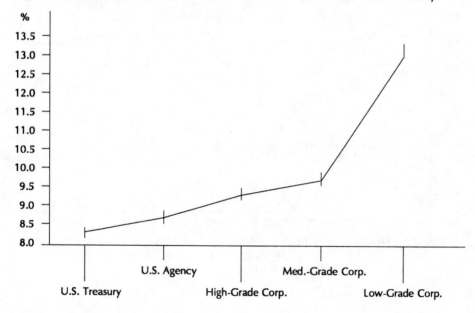

To keep a lid on the volume of data, we'll focus on what's referred to as the long end of the market. Municipal bonds will also be excluded, because their nontaxable status adds unneeded complications.

	U.S.	U.S.			
Mature	Treas.	Agency	High Corp.	Med. Corp.	Low Corp.
5 yr.	7.81%	8.10%	8.59%	9.47%	11.87%
10 yr.	8.23%	8.66%	9.29%	9.75%	13.00%
20 yr.	8.38%	9.09%	9.52%	10.03%	13.30%
30 yr.	8.49%	9.30%	9.81%	10.34%	13.69%

COMPARATIVE YIELD RATES

Now we can create a current profile of the market's current risk perception. We can then relate the risk perceived in Sample's transaction to the market profile to converge on a discount rate.

Let's add a sublabel to the column headings for the risk categories:

Market:	U.S. Treas.	U.S. Agency	High Corp.	Med. Corp.	Low Corp.
Target:	Risk-Free	Lowest Risk	Some Risk	Norm Risk	High Risk

Classification of the target company is undoubtedly subjective, but we can still approach it with objective tools.

Weighted Risk Grade

Using the Value Components, we can evaluate the overall risk by weighting each component and grading the risk for each. Summing the weighted grades will provide an index number, which can be related to a risk category, which can be related to a market yield and, finally, in turn to a discount rate.

Component Weight

Components should be weighted as:

Most important: Those components that are the real make-or-break items. Failure means ruin. Overall business success requires success with these components. Weight: 3.

Important: Key components for which failure truly devalues the enterprise, while success with the component means a major boost to overall success of the enterprise. Weight: 2

Meaningful: Other components whose outcome has a material effect. Weight: 1

Immaterial: Those components which, while perhaps interesting, do not make much difference in the long run. Weight: 0.

Criticisms and Responses

Three possible criticisms and their necessary responses are as follows:

Criticism #1:   In fact, a poor enough performance in any one area of operations may mean ruin. As an area deteriorates, it becomes more pressing to focus on that component, as every component might ultimately deserve a Weight of 3.

Response: What we are dealing with is a company poised in the real world on the brink of its future. It is in a particular economy, industry, location, and the like, all of which have distinct, ascertainable characteristics right now. There are differences in priorities that spring from the characteristics. If all components had the same weight, there would be no way to consider the relative importance each bears to the others.

Criticism #2:   Maybe there's not enough differentiation with only four categories. One cannot achieve an adequate degree of refinement.

Response: Too many levels are likely to add too much complexity to what should be a simple-to-use tool. We are striving to aid judgment on a final subjective decision. It is self-deluding to believe arithmetic precision can substitute for business judgment itself.

Criticism #3:   Over time, the potential impact of all these components will almost certainly change. Weighting now may be misleading.

Response: The market deals with the here and now. We cannot obtain money for purchase today at a cost of capital of 5 percent just because there may be a day in the future when the market will be asking only 5 percent for funds in our risk category. The market yield today is shaped by the world of today, of which the target is a part and in which it must be measured and judged.

Risk Grades are assigned on a scale of +3 to –3:

+3 = Virtually certain to be a positive outcome

+2 = Strong likelihood of a positive outcome

+1 = Above average likelihood of a positive outcome

 0 = Normal Risk

−1 = Above average likelihood of a negative outcome

−2 = Strong likelihood of a negative outcome

−3 = Virtually certain to be a negative outcome

"Outcome" means that events of the component are expected to have a positive or negative effect *on the target company*. If inflation rises, it will likely be a negative for a company like Sample facing resistance in raising its own prices. But for another company with long-term fixed-price supply contracts (holding the company's costs constant while it remains free to raise prices in tune with the general market) this is more probably a positive.

Let's run through a grading exercise for Sample, based on what we've already learned:

Component	Weight	Raw Grade	Weighted Grade
Personnel	2	+1	+2
Customers	2	−1	−2
Relationships	1	+1	+1
Tangible Assets	1	0	0
Intangibles	0	0	0
Liabilities	0	0	0
Tax Attributes	0	−1	0
Research & Development	0	0	0
Gross National Product	3	−1	−3
Inflation	1	−2	−2
Industry	3	+1	+3
Interest Rates	2	−1	−2
International	0	0	0
Technology	0	−2	0
Competition	3	−1	−3
Regulation	0	−1	0
Social Taste	0	0	0
Political	1	0	0
Resources	2	−3	−6
Labor	3	+1	+3
Totals	24		−9
Final Weighted Risk Grade			−0.375

Some explanations are in order abut this grading before we move on to using the results.

Even though the weighted risk grade for some components multiplies out to zero, those zero-weighted components still get a grade for two reasons. First, because weights might change upon review. Secondly, and more importantly, because grading highlights issues that might alert the analyst for the future. They thereby help to create a more detailed backdrop against which business judgment can be more confidently applied.

Because the weighted risk grade is a multiple, a zero in either column produces a zero product. That shouldn't be surprising, as anything other than zero has been predefined as a deviation from *normal* risk. The system seeks normality; it wants abnormality to strain to make itself heard. Abnormality must prove it is a material, outstanding deviation.

Along the same lines, the zeroes (normal risk) in the raw grade when multiplied against a nonzero weight priority have the effect of diluting the impact of nonzero grades. So, when interpreting results and preparing to make the subjective decision, the unusually high weighted grades—like Resources with –6 in our example—deserve to be kept in mind. They may properly influence the analyst's ultimate exercise of business judgment.

Discount Rate: Decision

The final weighted risk grade relates to the market yields in this way, shown in the table on page 123.

Maturity figures in as the time frame the investment in the business will be maintained by the buyer. For all practical purposes, a 30-year period is viewed as indefinite.

To settle on a Market Yield, one can interpolate, or merely round to the nearest whole number, depending upon the subjective preference of the analyst. If the weighted grade is worse than –1, the analyst may well wish to add something more to the High Risk Market Yield, perhaps even multiplying by the absolute value of the weighted risk grade.

For example, if the weighted grade were –2, the super-High Risk Market Yield (30-year) could be calculated as:

$$(2)(13.69\%) = 27.38\%!$$

Now, one final step to make the jump from Market Yield to Discount

WEIGHTED RISK GRADE TO MARKET YIELD

Market:	U.S. Treasury	U.S. Agency	High-Grade Corporate	Medium-Grade Corporate	Low-Grade Corporate
Target:	Risk-Free	Lowest Risk	Some Risk	Normal Risk	High Risk
Weight Grade:	+3	+2	+1	0	−1
5 Year	7.81%	8.10%	8.59%	9.47%	11.87%
10 Year	8.23%	8.66%	9.29%	9.75%	13.00%
20 Year	8.38%	9.09%	9.52%	10.03%	13.30%
30 Year	8.49%	9.30%	9.81%	10.34%	13.69%

Rate. We need this last jump because the Market Yield information developed so far is applicable to *debt* securities. The Discount Rate will be used for an *equity* value.

Of course, equity is riskier than debt. There is no specific time for repayment, nor promise of repayment. Debt securities have the higher legal claim on assets. Debt at issuance promises a specific Stream of Income; equity does not. Debt may be specifically secured and immovable in its priority claim on assets, even if new debt (which still comes ahead of equity) is created. Equity on the other hand, is prone to dilution by the issuance of any new equity.

When risk is higher, reward must be higher to compensate, so the discount rate for equity ought to exceed the Market Yield for debt. Now the $64 question: By how much?!?

As a general rule-of-thumb, equity runs at 1.5 times debt rates. At the low-risk end of the scale one might find less of a premium, while at the very high-risk end (beyond –1) it may run somewhat higher, even 2 or 3 times the already high yield rate. Of course, any of these rates can be converted to a PE ratio by reciprocation.

So a completed chart for an indefinite time frame would look like this shown in the table on page 125.

More often than not multiples are rounded to the nearest 0.5 times, but the above chart uses the precise reciprocal to duplicate the effects of the equity rate.

Discount Rate: Confirmation

Do these Discount Rates work? For our –0.375 risk graded target company, we would be looking at an interpolated rate of about 17.4 percent or a PE Ratio of 5.75 times. That's the rate we settle on: 17.4%.

Back in Chapter 3, capitalization rates were discussed as a function of buyer goals, presumably based on the buyer's cost of capital. Also, we mentioned Comparison Values as a potential method for valuation. We will weave those two concepts into the verification procedure.

As the business price and the discount rate must always be a product of the marketplace, those two hard-ground baselines should confirm the subjective decision derived from the sophisticated mathematics used above. If they do not, the "bugs" have to be found and corrected.

Because the marketplace and each of its players are vulnerable to shifts in psychology, emotions, and imperfect information, it is quite possible that what a company *should* sell for (the mathematical value) will not be the same as what it *will* sell for (the transaction price).

Market:	U.S. Treasury	U.S. Agency	High-Grade Corporate	Medium-Grade Corporate	Low-Grade Corporate
Target:	Risk-Free	Lowest Risk	Some Risk	Normal Risk	High Risk
Weight Grade:	+3	+2	+1	0	–1
30 Year	8.49%	9.30%	9.81%	10.34%	13.69%
Premium	1.25X	1.33X	1.50X	1.50X	1.50X
Equity Rate	10.61%	12.40%	14.72%	15.51%	20.53%
PE Ratio:	9.42X	8.06X	6.80X	6.45X	4.87X

As a buyer can decide his acceptable cap rate (discount rate, PE ratio, multiplier, and so forth, he's free to accept or reject each deal, though the prudent buyer will presumably exercise care and skill in making the decision.

The seller's task is somewhat tougher. The business the seller has is the only one he can sell. What is a wise cap rate for the seller?

In discussing Comparison Values, we talked about market PE rates and cautioned that publicly traded stock often seems rather divorced in value from the comparable privately held entity. Greater liquidity and the peculiarities of the market, speculation, and information flow can produce a very different picture than would exist in the closely held environment. The other problem encountered in trying to use stock market data is its volatility, which often makes the figures too much of a moving target.

Hence, data for other privately held companies in the same industry may be more useful. Trade associations, government agencies, credit reporting companies, and banking industry sources are more likely to have information that is free from those disadvantages. The information from those quarters often can be broken down by various measures of size—by location, by industry subdivision, or by other features—making a reliable comparison more probable and more easily discernible.

Adjustment for risk is still a vital consideration. The twist, though, is to now make that adjustment in light of normal risk for the companies to which the target is being compared. After all, their own implicit rates already incorporate the standard risks as perceived by the marketplace. What we want to know is where the target fits in that scheme.

The final piece of confirmation, for both buyer and seller, is the relationship to the cost of capital, as will ultimately be reflected in the financing arrangements for the transaction. While the seller usually does not have an offer to work with when setting a price, the seller should theorize what a likely offer will be, based on what a bank (or the seller directly) is willing to lend as a percentage of the proposed transaction price and determine a rate (or rates) for the potential loan(s).

Let us say, for example, the seller's analysis so far suggests a price of $1 million. Then:

$$(17.4\%)\,(\$1,000,000) = \$174,000$$

Is the business going to generate $174,000 per year in profits? If not, the price is out of line or we've chosen the wrong rate. If confirmation is not achieved, we have to find the "bugs."

Note, importantly, all the figures we have been dealing with on this score are pretax, including the rates of return. (The exemption from state income tax of U.S. Government obligations is here assumed to be negligible.)

But hold on a minute! What if the buyer can leverage the transaction? Most buyers will indeed want some leverage if the cost of funds is acceptable. Many buyers will, in fact, be priced out of the market without some debt because they cannot afford to come up with so much equity in an upfront lump sum.

We check with our local banker who tells us the bank will lend up to half the price to a qualified buyer at 2 percent over the Prime Rate. Prime is currently at 8.5 percent, so a buyer is looking at 10.5 percent for the cost of debt. There's going to be just one class of stock. The cost of capital then will be 13.95 percent.

	Amount	**Cost**	**Service**
Debt Capital:	$500,000	10.50%	$52,500
Equity Capital:	500,000	17.40%	$87,000
Total Capital:	$1,000,000	13.95%	$139,500

Now we only need $139,500 per year in profits to justify the million-dollar price tag. And that's because we are now able to use a blended cost of capital discount rate equivalent of 13.95 percent.

Parenthetically, it is implicit that the equity portion rate is a minimum acceptable rate to the buyer. If 17.4 percent were a true cost, we would need something more in return to give the investor a profit. In reality, the cost to the buyer is an opportunity cost of not being able to employ the capital elsewhere. (The terminology in this area can be very tricky.)

We can drop the rate further and raise the price (assuming projected annual profits still work out to $139,500) if the seller wants to supplant or supplement the bank as lender. Seller-financed businesses usually carry a higher *stated* price tag, but the true value of the transaction to the seller is lowered by the risk of buyer default, and, may be lowered further if the seller subsidizes the buyer by accepting a lower interest rate on the takeback debt than the seller could earn by investing elsewhere. The precise effect on the seller's price is a function of the differential in interest rates and the repayment schedule.

In defense of seller takebacks, even at sweetheart rates, it is worth noting there may be certain tax advantages in deferring receipt of full payment under Installment Sale Provisions of the Internal Revenue Code.

Further, so long as the seller can exercise audit and inspection rights to keep the buyer from gutting the business, the seller is in a better position to repossess than a banker, because the seller's experience should certainly make him the most capable of running the business and preserving operations and value.

It is not surprising then that many sellers are comfortable with, even eager for, a takeback deal. Consideration of takeback financing arrangements as an alternative may literally suggest more than one asking price, and may serve as a wonderful tool in successfully negotiating a deal.

THE PRICE

With the risk and adjustment problems solved, it is now just a matter of plugging into the chosen formulas. Those were detailed in Chapter 3, together with a discussion of the pluses and minuses of each. Rarely will they yield a uniform figure. Price choices will vary, but they will collectively stake out a range. Often a majority will cluster within a relatively narrow sector of that range.

Let's see how things finally stack up for Sample Company.

DECISIONAL CALCULATIONS

We'll attack the final solution in three steps:

1. Determine a preferred clinical value from our range of potential values developed using all the different methods. The preferred value can be an average or any other figure, within the range. It does not have to equal exactly one of the calculated values.

2. Adjust the preferred clinical value to obtain a tentative price.

3. Test and make final adjustments for a final price.

To get things underway, let's review the list of clinical values we found in our examination of all the methods:

Method	Clinical Value	Hi-Lo Rank
Asset Based:		
Book Value	$297,760	13 (Lowest)
Adjusted Book Value	$391,844	11
Present Net Asset Growth Value	$416,000	9
Replacement Value	$479,244	6

Method	Clinical Value	Hi-Lo Rank
Start-up Value	N/A	
Stream-of-Income Based:		
5-Year Payback Value	$399,751	10
PE Ratio Value	$377,807	12
10-Year Discounted Income Value	$540,771	4
Combination Methods:		
Excess Income Plus Assets	$434,480	8
Total Present Value	$641,148	2
Marketplace Methods:		
Prior Sales	$500,000	5
Comparable Value	$453,368	7
Market-to-Book	$584,919	3
Revenue Multiplier	$814,474	1 (Highest)
Average*	$487,044	A
Median*	$453,368	M

*Excludes Start-up from averaging calculations.

Plugging the numbers into a range line, to give us an idea of cluster, we see the range shown in the chart on page 130.

Sheer weight of numbers suggests a price of around $400,000; the average is showing up around $500,000. Recent sales have also gone off at $500,000, which is a powerful argument for that figure.

The favored rational method, Total Present Value, is higher at $640,000, which, excluding the anomalous Revenue Multiplier, is the highest. Ergo, this looks like a suggested price for the seller.

It is worth noting the cluster at $400m is made up of four different types of methods, lacking only a representative from the marketplace classification. Those are powerful arguments for the buyer.

Is it going to be possible to get the two together? Should they?

If the projections are agreed upon, and if we use the cost of capital figures of 17.4 percent for equity, 10.5 percent for debt, and a blended rate (assuming one-half financed) of 13.95 percent, how will the buyer fare at the three possibilities? (We are focusing on *pretax* profits.) Let's take a look at how the buyer would have done in 19X7 (the latest year) and at just 19X8, as the figures get more and more speculative as we move further out:

Figure 5.3: Clinical Range Cluster

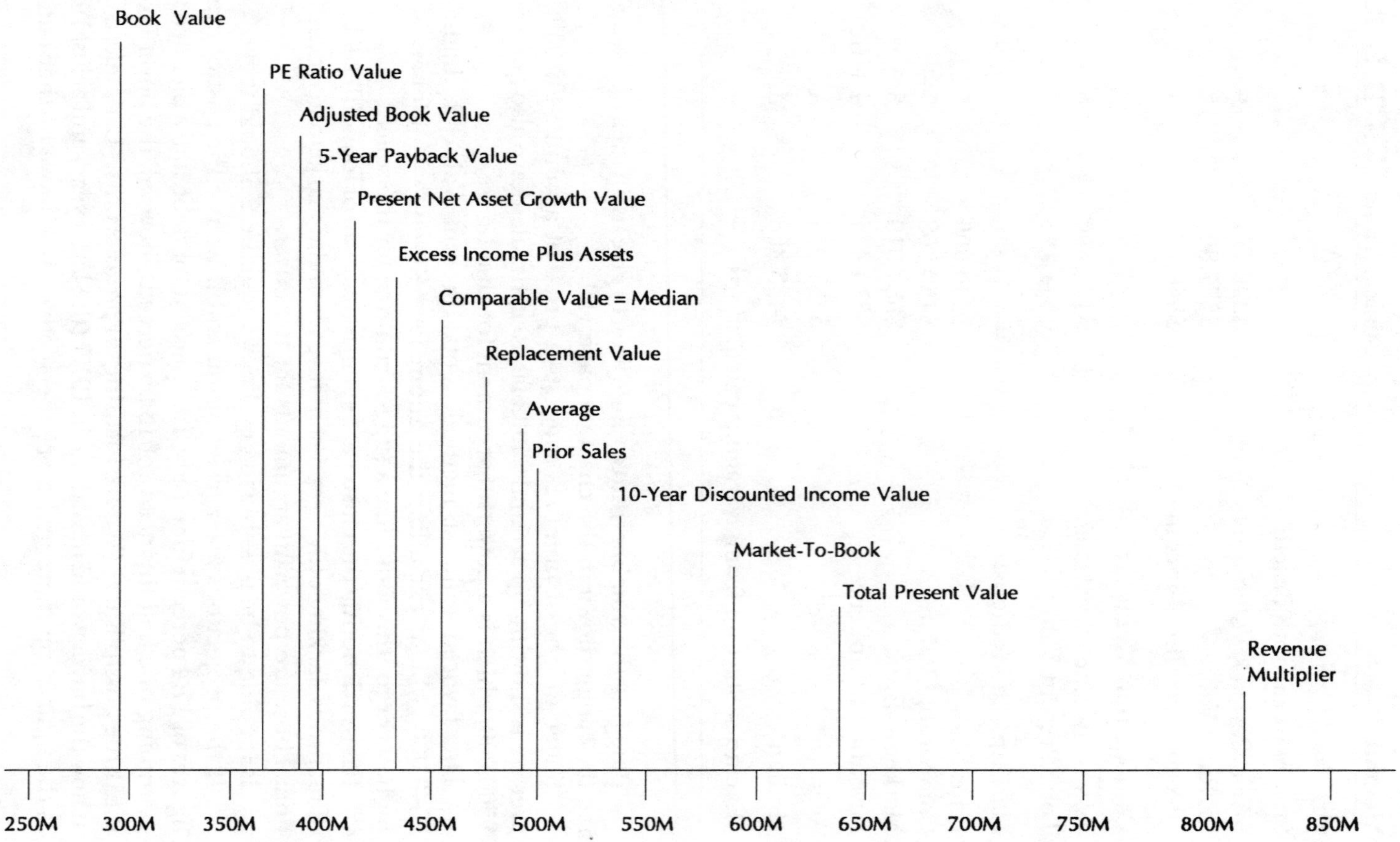

	Price Alternative	Profit	Rate of Return	13.95%+(−)
Alt. #1: 19X7	400,000	88,383	22.10%	+8.15%
19X8	400,000	82,613	20.65%	+6.70%
Alt. #2: 19X7	500,000	88,383	17.68%	+3.73%
19X8	500,000	82,613	16.52%	+2.57%
Alt. #3: 19X7	640,000	88,383	13.81%	−0.14%
19X8	640,000	82,613	12.91%	−1.04%

Based on this information, it's pretty clear the seller is going to have to come down some. Is there a "bug" in the numbers?

Yes, of sorts. Remember when the seller's rational numbers were calculated, a discount rate of only 15 percent was estimated. We've since seen that a more appropriate rate is 17.4 percent (or thereabouts). If that figure is used as a discount rate we'll come up with an adjusted Total Present Value of $563,298. Given the two figures for Total Present Value, the seller may want to build in a little cushion and ask around the mid-range of $600,000. He might signal a willingness to settle for less by using a figure of $595,000, though it's the extraordinary buyer who will meet the asking price and the extraordinary seller who won't bend a bit on price. The parties are getting closer.

The 17.4 percent discount rate presumably compensates for risk, but there are a number of factors here which may make even this price a little rich for a buyer. The earnings history is erratic. Sample has had regular problems in controlling overhead. Its equipment and vehicles are fairly old and will probably need to be replaced soon. A significant portion of the business, the sale of merchandise, is turning in a static performance. And then there's that nagging zoning problem, which by itself may mean knocking off $30,000 from the value of assets.

On the other hand, the projections seem to make sense. The company has three reasonably good years behind it. Fresh ownership might be just the tonic to get the overhead problems under control and make some really significant profits with improved operating leverage.

If the seller can accept it, a price on the order of $520,000 would appear to be the best price based on reasonable business judgment.

Can the seller accept $520,000? In part, that will depend on what the seller invested originally. What it really depends upon is the intensity of desire we talked about, for both the seller and buyer. Odds are, though, for Sample, if the business stays on the market, performance continues apace, and market conditions remain stable, $520,000 will be at or very near the final price. (Note it provides the Buyer a 15.89% ROR in 19X8; above the Buyer's 15% minimum, but not extraordinarily higher.)

The decision then:

Seller's Asking Price:	$600,000
Buyer's Offer Price:	$400,000
Likely Transaction Price:	$520,000

SPECIAL CASES

There are a few kinds of business circumstances that at first blush may not *seem* to fit the normal course of analysis. In fact, they do fit, but a little extra thought, and some extra care are usually needed.

The "One-Man Show"

Many small businesses are largely an extension of the owner. Take him or her out of the picture and what do you have? Just some liquidatable assets? Such denigration of value is especially common in the professions. Is there any worth over the salvage value of assets?

Yes, Virginia, there usually is more worth than just salvage. Some customers will continue to do business with the company, and that stream of revenue is the key to value. But it is a revenue stream destined to decline, not grow, in the absence of the key person. Any growth will be a product of the buyer's own ability, which the buyer shouldn't have to pay extra for. The question is how fast will revenue decline? Put another way, what is the expected decay rate?

For example, say a one-person consulting business is grossing $200,000 per year. Direct costs are negligible, since they're just the owner's time involvement. Overhead, however, adds up to $50,000 per year. There's $10,000 in business assets, mainly some office furniture and a personal computer with software. Files and source materials are worth, at most, another $5,000.

Now, let's say our consultant has decided to retire and is casting around for a buyer qualified both in financial terms and in terms of taking over the consulting practice. First the owner must predict a decay rate. After examining the amount of repeat business and reviewing the customer list, he determines a 50 percent annual dropout rate in the absence of any new marketing efforts.

Accordingly, the projections work out this way:

Year	Revenue	Overhead	Profit
1	200,000	50,000	150,000
2	100,000	50,000	50,000
3	50,000	50,000	0
4	25,000	50,000	−25,000

Now if we continue the projections, the losses would grow and grow, with no end in sight. Of course, the prudent businessperson would fold the business in that case. So, then, all we're talking about is a 2-year revenue stream plus the $15,000, give or take, of assets. It may be a small revenue stream, but it has a value, which can be priced out just like any other set of projections.

The Loss-Ridden Company

A company showing frequent or continuous losses will project out as a negative if its prior history is simply extrapolated into the future. The solution should be obvious. Don't extrapolate. Project. If projections, too, are negative, the owner shouldn't keep hitting his head against a stone wall. It makes sense to go out of business and stop the bleeding. Salvage value of the assets, which may well include some decay-rated value for a customer list, is going to be the economic worth of the business.

But if there's a solid revenue base and a reasonable business concept, see what the business will be worth if it can be turned around. Discount rates will surely be higher to compensate for the higher risk. Net assets may be reduced more than normally for contingencies. Other value decrements may be embraced; but a price can be set, justified and transacted.

The Brand-New Company

How about an outfit with no business history? Just like the loss-ridden outfit, we want to focus on the future, albeit with an emphasis on adjustment for risk. But we can find a price.

This situation is also a natural for a close look at the less frequently used methods of Replacement Value and Start-up Value. Those methods should marks the lower end of the range as a core value.

Publicly Held Companies

Many of the mathematical models will be defied by the market price of publicly traded stock. Which is correct?

The market calls the shots and it is the undeniable price of the moment. Note, though, the slew of public companies that have "gone private" or been bought out at substantial premiums above market price. They bear out the earlier observations that for all its efficiency the marketplace does not always choose a price a company should sell at.

Foreign Companies

Trading, commercial, and accounting practices vary throughout the world. Currency fluctuations add to complexity of analysis. Laws may restrict ownership, thereby restricting the ready market and the real demand. Do the same pricing principles apply?

Yes, but the key here is more often than not to do extensive legwork to see what's really at the bottom line. An important footnote here is the definition of the bottom line, for currency controls, taxes, and disinvestment laws may substantially limit the amount one is able to repatriate. The result is there may be two (or more) returns to be calculated. One would be the internal business rate, while the second might be a substantially different (even negative) return to investors. There may be more, because in some countries investors may be categorized based on many factors, each category being entitled to different "privileges" of capital withdrawal.

Once a clarified bottom line is projectable, and true net assets ascertained, it's the same ball game. Once again, risk adjustment must be emphasized, for exchange rate changes at minimum, to any number of political and other component possibilities.

Less Than the Whole Company

What if a seller is offering only a piece of the business, not 100 percent. If the business is going to remain in one piece, but with more owners, is the sum of the parts equal to the whole?

No question, the whole must first be evaluated to get a handle on the big picture. Then the terms of the piece sale must be considered. The biggest question is control, but it is not the only one. Can the interest be freely resold? Who gets dividends, cash flow, or other distributions? Who gets any tax benefits? Who has what rights on future sale, merger, or liquidation? Who has what responsibilities? Most importantly: How are decisions made? Who's in control? Who's in charge? With proration of the whole to the piece as a baseline, adjustment for risk and expected return proceeds in the normal fashion, substantially dependent upon the answers to the foregoing kinds of questions.

Spin-offs and Split-ups

These events are the flip side of the piece of the business question. The classic situation is the sale of a division or a particular activity.

The key to the solution for this puzzle is to define the portion being sold as a business unto itself and evaluate from there in the usual manner. The hard part is isolating the respective parts, people, activities, customers, markets, assets, and liabilities.

Once again, depending upon the nature of the operations and the history of the integrated company, risk may be increased, especially if any of the different segments of the business were relying heavily on another for sales referrals, and/or if any were subsidizing the costs of another by offering underpriced services.

Uncommon Stock

Most of the analysis has focused on common stock, but that is not the only type of equity. Preferred stock, convertible preferred, convertible debt, classes of common, warrants, rights, units, letter stock, options, and preference stock all have claims or potential claims on equity. Many of these hybrids and mutants are rarely found in the privately held company, but that does not necessarily mean they might not be more widely used.

Again, the starting place is the whole business itself. Once that baseline price is set, determine where the particular security fits into the overall scheme, what rights it will have, the extent of the control it may exercise, and, finally, what return it is projected to produce. Then proceed normally.

The Shell Company

How about the company that has ceased operations? Generally, it sounds like a pure asset play, so check up on Liquidating, Replacement, and Start-up Values. But if the name still carries some goodwill (say it has a customer following, perhaps because of location), the potential revenue stream if operations are restarted (with the cost of restart factored in as a decrement to assets) may increase the price. The potential revenue stream will probably be subject to decay rate computations.

CONCLUSION

Despite all the quantification, it is true that the evaluation, pricing, and structuring of transactions are subject to a great degree of controversy, because the business value is always a moving target in a changing environment, salted with dynamic risks and impelling opportunities.

What separates success from failure and accuracy from error? The best analysts are those whose business judgment, honed and educated by the quantifications, leads them into fair and economically viable transactions. In that respect, the chemistry of the participants is often the most critical and the most mysterious factor in this crucial exercise of human enterprise.

Appendix 1

Sample Company

Financial Statements, Operating Statistics, and Profit Projections

SAMPLE COMPANY: 7-YEAR BALANCE SHEETS

	19X1	19X2	19X3	19X4	19X5	19X6	19X7	7-Year Totals	7-Year Average
Assets:									
Current:									
Cash & Equivalents	23252	31209	37249	16206	46801	57183	55646	267546	38221
Accts Receivable	139830	127139	131872	123483	139015	179972	202740	1044051	149150
Bad Debt Reserve	-4051	-3550	-4948	-3286	-7135	-7697	-7679	-38346	-5478
Inventory	38367	38786	40151	55663	58101	56114	72746	359928	51418
Misc. Receivables	7582	17602	9628	8629	5780	7575	10213	67009	9573
Prepaid Expenses	3449	6826	5237	6574	4532	6440	8267	41145	5878
Total Current	208429	218012	219189	207269	246914	299587	341933	1741333	248762
Fixed:									
Real Estate	94582	94582	94582	105982	105982	105982	105982	707674	101096
Equipment & Fixtures	54826	56611	61599	62547	72910	89235	108835	506563	72366
Vehicles	9564	9564	2610	2610	2610	2610	2610	32178	4597
Accum Deprec	-83599	-96921	-104287	-119179	-136140	-156370	-180520	-877016	-125288
Total Fixed	75373	63836	54504	51960	45362	41457	36907	369399	52771

Misc. Assets:

Life Ins. Cash Value	13321	15112	16771	18416	20046	21605	22943	128214	18316
Loans:									
Life Ins.	0	0	-10000	-8000	-5000	0	0	-23000	-3286
Patent	17000	17000	17000	17000	17000	17000	17000	119000	17000
Amortization of Patent	-1000	-2000	-3000	-4000	-5000	-6000	-7000	-28000	-4000
Total Misc.	29321	30112	20771	23416	27046	32605	32943	196214	28031
Total Assets	313123	311960	294464	282645	319322	373649	411783	2306946	329564

Liabs. & Equity:

Current Liabs.:

Accts. Payable	32945	23578	21355	30249	36543	42831	41170	228671	32667
Accrued Tax & Exp.	31680	15770	20114	17097	27149	32269	28216	172295	24614
Total Current Liabilities	64625	39348	41469	47346	63692	75100	69386	400966	57281

Debt Financing:

Bank Debt	0	29320	9000	15000	23750	16400	10000	103470	14781
Mortgage Payable	65844	61818	57136	52132	46781	41060	34637	359408	51344
Total Debt Financing	65844	91138	66136	67132	70531	57460	44637	462878	66125
Total Liabilities	130469	130486	107605	114478	134223	132560	114023	863844	123406

SAMPLE COMPANY: 7-YEAR BALANCE SHEETS (Continued)

	19X1	19X2	19X3	19X4	19X5	19X6	19X7	7-Year Totals	7-Year Average
Equity:									
Capital Stock	18800	18800	18800	18800	18800	18800	18800	131600	18800
Paid-in Surplus	29804	29804	29804	29804	29804	29804	29804	208628	29804
Retained Earnings	172993	171813	177198	158506	175438	231428	288099	1375478	196496
Treasury Stock	-38943	-38943	-38943	-38943	-38943	-38943	-38943	-272601	-38943
Total Equity	182654	181474	186859	168167	185099	241089	297760	1443102	206157
Total Liabilities & Equity	313123	311960	294464	282645	319322	373649	411783	2306946	329564

SAMPLE COMPANY: 7-YEAR INCOME STATEMENTS

	19X1	19X2	19X3	19X4	19X5	19X6	19X7	7-Year Totals	7-Year Average
Sales:									
Merchandise	554020	395961	373954	391042	470529	505071	517206	3207783	458255
Services	456713	554204	521744	518541	724936	847729	1114730	4738597	676942
Gross Sales	1010733	950165	895698	901338	1195465	1352800	1631936	7938165	1134019
Less: Returns/ Allowances	-2356	-1609	-1557	-1776	-2654	-3117	-2989	-16058	-2294
Net Sales	1008377	948556	894141	899562	1192811	1349683	1628947	7922077	1131725
Cost of Sales:									
Open Inventory	53198	38367	38786	40151	55663	58101	56114	340380	48626
Purchases	303916	262607	246269	277063	336561	313979	361946	2102341	300334
Close Inventory	38367	38786	40151	55663	58101	56114	72746	359928	51418
Merchandise Cost	318747	262188	244904	261551	334123	315966	345314	2082793	297542
Direct Labor	389422	414803	378033	372375	524175	571945	758855	3409608	487087
Total Cost Sales	708169	676991	622967	633926	858298	887911	1104169	5492401	784629
Gross Profit	300208	271565	271204	265636	334513	461772	524778	2429676	347097
Overhead:									
Officer Salaries	59791	63840	59364	64359	63502	67582	79260	457698	65385

141

SAMPLE COMPANY: 7-YEAR INCOME STATEMENTS (Continued)

	19X1	19X2	19X3	19X4	19X5	19X6	19X7	7-Year Totals	7-Year Average
Other Salaries	81749	71427	65890	70298	77229	114679	126629	607901	86843
Advertising & Promotion	4561	4881	5671	5212	3414	3842	6363	33944	4849
Bad Debts	1355	82	5602	2807	844	2681	1773	15144	2163
Consultants	12899	2240	2662	2365	1566	1175	1075	23982	3426
Depreciation	14288	13322	14320	14892	16961	20230	24150	118163	16880
Amortization	1000	1000	1000	1000	1000	1000	1000		
Insurance	5645	11849	10434	10839	12742	14173	14310	79992	11427
Legal & Accounting	7306	12242	9865	8856	8668	9863	8012	64812	9259
Miscellaneous	2508	5185	541	1566	579	877	2222	13478	1925
Office Expense	6598	7897	8136	8648	7136	8087	11788	58290	8327
Rents	3600	3600	3600	3600	3600	3600	3600	25200	3600
Repair & Maintenance	1283	1106	1493	3553	1738	2427	1138	12738	1820
Taxes—Payroll	14609	34537	32858	39423	52570	62946	71407	30835	44050
Taxes—Other	4205	4424	4366	3693	4553	5334	7723	34298	4900
Telephone	4833	4606	4908	5817	7518	8722	13916	50320	7189
Travel & Entertainment	11899	12050	11030	11770	11523	13241	16738	88251	12607
Utilities	2602	2513	2515	3524	3299	4403	7150	26006	3715
Vehicle Exp.	11327	14801	20462	21167	26046	27895	31282	152980	21854
Total Overhead	252058	271602	264717	283389	304488	372757	429536	2178547	311211
Operating Profit	48150	-37	6487	-17753	30025	89015	95242	251129	35876
Other Income	6344	3824	6962	1451	244	492	2792	22109	3158

	19X1	19X2	19X3	19X4	19X5	19X6	19X7	7-Year Total	7-Year Average
Interest Expense	4742	5300	5770	5689	5730	5362	9651	42244	6035
Pretax Profit	49752	-1513	7679	-21991	24539	84145	88383	230994	32999
Income Taxes	8349	-333	2294	-3299	7607	28155	31712	74485	10641
Net Profit	41403	-1180	5385	-18692	16932	55990	56671	156509	22358

SAMPLE COMPANY: PERCENTAGES OF SALES

	19X1	19X2	19X3	19X4	19X5	19X6	19X7	7-Year Total	7-Year Average
Net Sales	100.00	1000.00	100.00	100.00	100.00	100.00	100.00	100.00	100.00
Total Cost of Sales	70.23	71.37	69.67	70.47	71.96	65.79	67.78	69.33	69.33
Gross Profit	29.77	28.63	30.33	29.53	28.04	34.21	32.22	30.67	30.67
Overhead	25.00	28.63	29.61	31.50	25.53	27.62	26.37	27.50	27.50
Operating Profit	4.77	0.00	.73	-1.97	2.52	6.60	5.85	3.17	3.17
Pretax Profit	4.93	-.16	.86	-2.44	2.06	6.23	5.43	2.92	2.92
Taxes	.83	-.04	.26	-.37	.64	2.09	1.95	.94	.94
Net Profit	4.11	-.12	.60	-2.08	1.42	4.15	3.48	1.98	1.98

SAMPLE COMPANY: 7-YEAR CASH FLOW STATEMENTS

	19X1	19X2	19X3	19X4	19X5	19X6	19X7	7-Year Total	7-Year Average
Cash Flow:									
+ Net Profit	41403	-1180	5385	-18692	16932	55990	56671	156509	22358
+ Depreciation & Amortization	14288	14322	15320	15892	17961	21230	25150	124163	17738
- Realty Purchases	0	0	0	11400	0	0	0	11400	1629
- Equipment Purchases	6000	1785	4988	948	10363	16325	19600	60009	8573
- Net Receivables Increase	11246	-12190	3335	-6727	11683	40395	22786	70528	10075
- Inventory Increase	-14831	419	1365	15512	2438	-1987	16632	19548	2793
Miscellaneous Receivables Increase	3014	10020	-7974	-999	-2849	1795	2638	5645	806
- Prepaids Increase	-2477	3377	-1589	1377	-2222	2088	1827	2341	334
- Life Insurance Increase	1041	1791	1659	1645	1630	1559	1338	10663	1523
+ Payables Increase	1729	-9367	-2223	8894	6294	6288	-1661	9954	1422
+ Accruals Increase	467	-15910	4344	-3017	10052	5120	-4053	-2997	-428

144

+ Net Loans Obtained	0	29320	10000	6000	8750	0	0	54070	7724
– Net Loan Repayment	3500	4026	25002	7004	8351	18071	12823	110277	15754
= Net Cash Flow	18894	7957	6040	–21043	30595	10382	–1537	51288	7327

Reconciliation:

Opening Cash Balance	4358	23252	31209	37249	16206	46801	57183
+ Net Cash Flow	18894	7957	6040	–21043	30595	10382	–1537
= Closing Cash Balance	23252	31209	37249	16206	46801	57183	55646

SAMPLE COMPANY: 10-YEAR PROFIT PROJECTIONS

Yr #	Year	Sales	Cost of Goods Sold	Gross Profit	Overhead	Net Interest	Pretax Profit	Taxes	Net Profits
0	19X7	1628947	1104169	524778	429536	6859	88383	31712	56671
		+10%/Y	69% sale	31% sale	+8%/yr	0.5% sale	Calc'd	35% pret	
1	19X8	1791842	1236371	555471	463899	8959	82613	28914	53699
2	19X9	1971026	1360008	611018	501011	9855	100152	35053	65099
3	19Y0	2168128	1496009	672120	541092	10841	120188	42066	78122
4	19Y1	2384941	1645609	739332	584379	11925	143028	50060	92968
5	19Y2	2623435	1810170	813265	631129	13117	169019	59156	109863
6	19Y3	2885779	1991187	894591	681620	14429	198543	69490	129053
7	19Y4	3174357	2190306	984051	736149	15872	232030	81210	150820
8	19Y5	3491793	2409337	1082456	795041	17459	269956	94484	175472
9	19Y6	3840972	2650271	1190701	858644	19205	312852	109498	203354
10	19Y7	4225069	2915298	1309771	927336	21125	361310	126459	234851

Appendix 2

Personnel Evaluation Statistics Template

INSTRUCTIONS

Use this template to develop a view of the personnel in the target company. Grade each statistic according to the key as a predictor of the attributes desired in the target's personnel. Those with high or medium correlation should be investigated to see how the workforce measures up.

Key: H = Probably high correlation, so good predictor.

M = Probably medium correlation, so worthwhile predictor.

L = Probably low correlation, so may have some predictive value.

N = Probably no correlation at all, so not usable as predictor.

D = Direct correlation; that is, higher the statistic, higher the quality manifestation.

I = Inverse correlation; that is, higher the statistic, lower the quality manifestation.

	Cohesive	Communicative	Competent	Creative	Dependable	Ethical	Honest	Self-Initiating	Loyal	Obedient	Productive	Stabel	Cost-Effective
Statistic													
Number of Employees													
Year: Manhours Worked													
Years of Education													
Training Completed													
High School Degrees													
College Degrees													
Post-Grad Degrees													
Age													
Years Work Experience													
Years Industry Experience													
Years of Company Experience													
# Customer Complaints													
# Customer Commends													
Annual Payroll $													
Average Payroll $													
Annual Benefit $													
Average Annual Benefit $													
Pension Participants													
Pension % Vested													
Average Pension Account													
Average Vested Pension													
Years to Normal Retirement													
# Unionized													
# Employee Shareholders													
# Restrictive Contracts													
Year: # Terminations													
Year: # Volun. Termin.													
Year: # Invol. Termin.													
Year: # Health Termin.													
Year: # Retirements													

	Cohesive	Communicative	Competent	Creative	Dependable	Ethical	Honest	Self-Initiating	Loyal	Obedient	Productive	Stabel	Cost-Effective
Year: # Early Retirement													
Year: # Deaths													
Turnover													
Year: # Days Absences													
Absenteeism Rate													
Year: # Labor Grievances													
Year: # Job Injuries													
Year: # Comp. Claims													
Year: # Contest Comp.													
Year: # Unemp. Claims													
Year: # Contest Unemp.													
Average Commute Distance													
Average Commute Time													
Sales/Employee													
Sales/Payroll $													
Sales/Manhour													
Assets/Employee													
Assets/Payroll $													
Assets/Manhour													
Output/Employee													
Output/Payroll $													
Output/Manhour													
Inventory/Employee													
Shrinkage/Employee													
Debt/Employee													
Profit/Employee													
Profit/Payroll $													
Profit/Manhour													
Cash Flow/Employee													
Cash Flow/Payroll $													
Cash Flow/Manhour													

Appendix 3

Mathematical Conventions

The following symbols and conventions are used to express mathematical operations and concepts:

$=$	Equals.
$+$	Addition (also means positive result).
$-$	Subtraction (also means negative result).
$(x)(y)$	Multiplication, i.e., x times y.
x/y	Division, i.e., x divided by y.
x^y	Exponent as x raised to the y power. (Exponent is shown as a superscript.)
$\ln x$	Common Logarithm, as the common logarithm of x.
$>$	Greater than.
$<$	Less than.
$\geq$	Greater than or equal to.
$\leq$	Less than or equal to.
...	Formula repeats with progressive change in variable(s).
n	A number (e.g., number of years).

$\sum_{x=1}^{n}$ Sum, as in sum of the numbers for variable x from 1 to n.

x_n Identification of a variable, e.g., the nth x. (The identifier is shown as a subscript.)

Appendix 4

Compendium of Formulas

The following formulas are cross-indexed to the page where first used in the book. See Appendix 3 for Mathematical Conventions.

Page   **Description and Formula**

47   Linear Curve:

$$y = a + (b)(x)$$

where:

  y = Dependent Variable
  x = Independent Variable
  a = First Constant
  b = Second Constant

47   Exponential Curve:

$$y = (a)(e)^{(b)(x)} \qquad (a > 0)$$

where:

y = Dependent Variable
x = Independent Variable
e = natural logarithmic base = approx. 2.71828
a = First Constant
b = Second Constant

47   Logarithmic Curve:

$$y = a + (b)(\ln x)$$

where:

y = Dependent Variable
$\ln x$ = Logarithm of the Independent Variable
a = First Constant
b = Second Constant

47   Power Curve:

$$y = (a)(x)^b \qquad (a > 0)$$

where:

y = Dependent Variable
x = Independent Variable
a = First Constant
b = Second Constant

58   Book Value:

$$\text{Total Assets} - \text{Total Liabilities}$$

66   Present Net Asset Growth Value:

$$\frac{(1 + G)^n (A)}{(1 + i)^n}$$

where:

n = Number of Years
G = Growth Rate
i = Discount Rate
A = Net Assets at time of analysis

73   Discounted Income Value:

$$\frac{x_1}{(1+i)^1} + \frac{x_2}{(1+i)^2} + \ldots + \frac{x_n}{(1+i)^n}$$

where:

x_n = Profit for year n
i = Discount Rate

73   PE Value:

(Price–Earnings Ratio)(Latest Earnings)

75   Excess Income Plus Assets:

$$E + \frac{(e-(S)(i))}{i}$$

where:

E = Current Equity
e = Earnings
S = Starting Equity
i = Normal Rate of Return

78   Total Present Value:

$$DIV + \frac{ABVm}{(1+i)^n}$$

where:

$$\text{DIV} = \text{Discounted Income Value (see above)}$$
$$\text{ABVm} = \text{Modified Adjusted Book Value}$$
$$i = \text{Discount Rate}$$
$$n = \text{Time Period}$$

80   Prior Sales:

(Shares Outstanding) (Transaction Price Per Share)

81   Market to Book:

(Company Book Value) ((Industry Market Value/Industry Book Value))

83   Revenue Multiplier Value:

(12 Mos. Sales) (Industry Multiplier)

Appendix 5

Present Value and Compound Interest Tables

Present Value of One Dollar: $PV_0 = FV_n \left[\dfrac{1}{(1 + i)^n} \right]$

where $\dfrac{1}{(1 + i)^n} = PVIF_{i,n}$ and is shown in the following table.

n	1%	2%	3%	4%	5%	6%	7%	8%	9%	10%	11%	12%	13%	14%	15%
1	0.99010	0.98039	0.97087	0.96154	0.95238	0.94340	0.93458	0.92593	0.91743	0.90909	0.90090	0.89286	0.88496	0.87719	0.86957
2	0.98030	0.96117	0.94260	0.92456	0.90703	0.89000	0.87344	0.85734	0.84168	0.82645	0.81162	0.79719	0.78315	0.76947	0.75614
3	0.97059	0.94232	0.91514	0.88900	0.86384	0.83962	0.81630	0.79383	0.77218	0.75131	0.73119	0.71178	0.69305	0.67497	0.65752
4	0.96098	0.92385	0.88849	0.85480	0.82270	0.79209	0.76290	0.73503	0.70843	0.68301	0.65873	0.63552	0.61332	0.59208	0.57175
5	0.95147	0.90573	0.86261	0.82193	0.78353	0.74726	0.71299	0.68058	0.64993	0.62092	0.59345	0.56743	0.54276	0.51937	0.49718
6	0.94204	0.88797	0.83748	0.79031	0.74622	0.70496	0.66634	0.63017	0.59627	0.56447	0.53464	0.50663	0.48032	0.45559	0.43233
7	0.93272	0.87056	0.81309	0.75992	0.71068	0.66506	0.62275	0.58349	0.54703	0.51316	0.48166	0.45235	0.42506	0.39964	0.37594
8	0.92348	0.85349	0.78941	0.73069	0.67684	0.62741	0.58201	0.54027	0.50187	0.46651	0.43393	0.40388	0.37616	0.35056	0.32690
9	0.91434	0.83675	0.76642	0.70259	0.64461	0.59190	0.54393	0.50025	0.46043	0.42410	0.39092	0.36061	0.33288	0.30751	0.28426
10	0.90529	0.82035	0.74409	0.67556	0.61391	0.55839	0.50835	0.46319	0.42241	0.38554	0.35218	0.32197	0.29459	0.26974	0.24718
11	0.89632	0.80426	0.72242	0.64958	0.58468	0.52679	0.47509	0.42888	0.38753	0.35049	0.31728	0.28748	0.26070	0.23662	0.21494
12	0.88745	0.78849	0.70138	0.62460	0.55684	0.49697	0.44401	0.39711	0.35553	0.31683	0.28584	0.25667	0.23071	0.20756	0.18691
13	0.87866	0.77303	0.68095	0.60057	0.53032	0.46884	0.41496	0.36770	0.32618	0.28966	0.25751	0.22917	0.20416	0.18207	0.16253
14	0.86996	0.75787	0.66112	0.57747	0.50507	0.44230	0.38782	0.34046	0.29925	0.26333	0.23199	0.20462	0.18068	0.15971	0.14133
15	0.86135	0.74301	0.64186	0.55526	0.48102	0.41726	0.36245	0.31524	0.27454	0.23939	0.20900	0.18270	0.15989	0.14010	0.12289
16	0.85282	0.72845	0.62317	0.53391	0.45811	0.39365	0.33873	0.29189	0.25187	0.21763	0.18829	0.16312	0.14150	0.12289	0.10686
17	0.84438	0.71416	0.60502	0.51337	0.43630	0.37136	0.31657	0.27027	0.23107	0.19784	0.16963	0.14564	0.12522	0.10780	0.09293
18	0.83602	0.70016	0.58739	0.49363	0.41552	0.35034	0.29586	0.25025	0.21199	0.17986	0.15282	0.13004	0.11081	0.09456	0.08080
19	0.82774	0.68643	0.57029	0.47464	0.39573	0.33051	0.27651	0.23171	0.19449	0.16351	0.13768	0.11611	0.09806	0.08295	0.07026
20	0.81954	0.67297	0.55367	0.45639	0.37689	0.31180	0.25842	0.21455	0.17843	0.14864	0.12403	0.10367	0.08678	0.07276	0.06110
21	0.81143	0.65978	0.53755	0.43883	0.35894	0.29415	0.24151	0.19866	0.16370	0.13513	0.11174	0.09256	0.07680	0.06383	0.05313
22	0.80340	0.64684	0.52189	0.42195	0.34185	0.27750	0.22571	0.18394	0.15018	0.12285	0.10067	0.08264	0.06796	0.05599	0.04620
23	0.79544	0.63414	0.50669	0.40573	0.32557	0.26180	0.21095	0.17031	0.13778	0.11168	0.09069	0.07379	0.06014	0.04911	0.04017
24	0.78757	0.62172	0.49193	0.39012	0.31007	0.24698	0.19715	0.15770	0.12640	0.10153	0.08170	0.06588	0.05322	0.04308	0.03493
25	0.77977	0.60953	0.47760	0.37512	0.29530	0.23300	0.18425	0.14602	0.11597	0.09230	0.07361	0.05882	0.04710	0.03779	0.03038

n	16%	17%	18%	19%	20%	21%	22%	23%	24%	25%	26%	27%	28%	29%	30%
1	0.86207	0.85470	0.84746	0.84034	0.83333	0.82645	0.81967	0.81301	0.80645	0.80000	0.79365	0.78740	0.78125	0.77519	0.76923
2	0.74316	0.73051	0.71818	0.70616	0.69444	0.68301	0.67186	0.66098	0.65036	0.64000	0.62988	0.62000	0.61035	0.60093	0.59172
3	0.64066	0.62437	0.60863	0.59342	0.57870	0.56447	0.55071	0.53738	0.52449	0.51200	0.49991	0.48819	0.47684	0.46583	0.45517
4	0.55229	0.53365	0.51579	0.49867	0.48225	0.46651	0.45140	0.43690	0.42297	0.40960	0.39675	0.38440	0.37253	0.36111	0.35013
5	0.47611	0.45611	0.43711	0.41905	0.40188	0.38554	0.37000	0.35520	0.34111	0.32768	0.31488	0.30268	0.29104	0.27993	0.26933
6	0.41044	0.38984	0.37043	0.35214	0.33490	0.31863	0.30328	0.28878	0.27509	0.26214	0.24991	0.23833	0.22737	0.21700	0.20718
7	0.35383	0.33320	0.31392	0.29592	0.27908	0.26333	0.24859	0.23478	0.22184	0.20972	0.19834	0.18766	0.17764	0.16822	0.15937
8	0.30503	0.28478	0.26604	0.24867	0.23257	0.21763	0.20376	0.19088	0.17891	0.16777	0.15741	0.14776	0.13878	0.13040	0.12259
9	0.26295	0.24340	0.22546	0.20897	0.19381	0.17986	0.16702	0.15519	0.14428	0.13422	0.12493	0.11635	0.10842	0.10109	0.09430
10	0.22668	0.20804	0.19106	0.17560	0.16151	0.14864	0.13690	0.12617	0.11635	0.10737	0.09915	0.09161	0.08470	0.07836	0.07254
11	0.19542	0.17781	0.16192	0.14756	0.13459	0.12285	0.11221	0.10258	0.09383	0.08590	0.07869	0.07214	0.06617	0.06075	0.05580
12	0.16846	0.15197	0.13722	0.12400	0.11216	0.10153	0.09198	0.08339	0.07567	0.06872	0.06245	0.05680	0.05170	0.04709	0.04292
13	0.14523	0.12989	0.11629	0.10420	0.09346	0.08391	0.07539	0.06780	0.06103	0.05498	0.04957	0.04472	0.04039	0.03650	0.03302
14	0.12520	0.11102	0.09855	0.08757	0.07789	0.06934	0.06180	0.05512	0.04921	0.04398	0.03934	0.03522	0.03155	0.02830	0.02540
15	0.10793	0.09489	0.08352	0.07359	0.06491	0.05731	0.05065	0.04481	0.03969	0.03518	0.03122	0.02773	0.02465	0.02194	0.01954
16	0.09304	0.08110	0.07078	0.06184	0.05409	0.04736	0.04152	0.03643	0.03201	0.02815	0.02478	0.02183	0.01926	0.01700	0.01503
17	0.08021	0.06932	0.05998	0.05196	0.04507	0.03914	0.03403	0.02962	0.02581	0.02252	0.01967	0.01719	0.01505	0.01318	0.01156
18	0.06914	0.05925	0.05083	0.04367	0.03756	0.03235	0.02789	0.02408	0.02082	0.01801	0.01561	0.01354	0.01175	0.01022	0.00889
19	0.05961	0.05064	0.04308	0.03669	0.03130	0.02673	0.02286	0.01958	0.01679	0.01441	0.01239	0.01066	0.00918	0.00792	0.00684
20	0.05139	0.04328	0.03651	0.03084	0.02608	0.02209	0.01874	0.01592	0.01354	0.01153	0.00983	0.00839	0.00717	0.00614	0.00526
21	0.04430	0.03699	0.03094	0.02591	0.02174	0.01826	0.01536	0.01294	0.01092	0.00922	0.00780	0.00661	0.00561	0.00476	0.00405
22	0.03819	0.03162	0.02622	0.02178	0.01811	0.01509	0.01259	0.01052	0.00880	0.00738	0.00619	0.00520	0.00438	0.00369	0.00311
23	0.03292	0.02702	0.02222	0.01830	0.01509	0.01247	0.01032	0.00855	0.00710	0.00590	0.00491	0.00410	0.00342	0.00286	0.00239
24	0.02838	0.02310	0.01883	0.01538	0.01258	0.01031	0.00846	0.00695	0.00573	0.00472	0.00390	0.00323	0.00267	0.00222	0.00184
25	0.02447	0.01974	0.01596	0.01292	0.01048	0.00852	0.00693	0.00565	0.00462	0.00378	0.00310	0.00254	0.00209	0.00172	0.00142

Example The present value of $1.00 received 5 years from now, discounted at 10 percent, is $0.62 ($1.00 × 0.62092 = $0.62).

Present Value of an Annuity ($1): $PV_a = PMT \sum_{t=1}^{n} \left[\dfrac{1}{(1 + i)^t} \right]$

where $\sum_{t=1}^{n} \left(\dfrac{1}{(1 + i)^t} \right) = PVAIF_{i,n}$ and is shown in the following table.

n	1%	2%	3%	4%	5%	6%	7%	8%	9%	10%	11%	12%	13%	14%	15%
1	0.9901	0.9804	0.9709	0.9615	0.9524	0.9434	0.9346	0.9259	0.9174	0.9091	0.9009	0.8929	0.8850	0.8772	0.8696
2	1.9704	1.9416	1.9135	1.8861	1.8594	1.8334	1.8080	1.7833	1.7591	1.7355	1.7125	1.6901	1.6681	1.6467	1.6257
3	2.9410	2.8839	2.8286	2.7751	2.7233	2.6730	2.6243	2.5771	2.5313	2.4868	2.4437	2.4018	2.3612	2.3216	2.2832
4	3.9020	3.8077	3.7171	3.6299	3.5459	3.4651	3.3872	3.3121	3.2397	3.1699	3.1024	3.0374	2.9745	2.9137	2.8550
5	4.8535	4.7134	4.5797	4.4518	4.3295	4.2123	4.1002	3.9927	3.8896	3.7908	3.6959	3.6048	3.5172	3.4331	3.3522
6	5.7955	5.6014	5.4172	5.2421	5.0757	4.9173	4.7665	4.6229	4.4859	4.3553	4.2305	4.1114	3.9976	3.8887	3.7845
7	6.7282	6.4720	6.2302	6.0020	5.7863	5.5824	5.3893	5.2064	5.0329	4.8684	4.7122	4.5638	4.4226	4.2883	4.1604
8	7.6517	7.3254	7.0196	6.7327	6.4632	6.2098	5.9713	5.7466	5.5348	5.3349	5.1461	4.9676	4.7988	4.6389	4.4873
9	8.5661	8.1622	7.7861	7.4353	7.1078	6.8017	6.5152	6.2469	5.9852	5.7590	5.5370	5.3282	5.1317	4.9464	4.7716
10	9.4714	8.9825	8.7302	8.1109	7.7217	7.3601	7.0236	6.7101	6.4176	6.1446	5.8892	5.6502	5.4262	5.2161	5.0188
11	10.3677	9.7868	9.2526	8.7604	8.3064	7.8868	7.4987	7.1389	6.8052	6.4951	6.2065	5.9377	5.6869	5.4527	5.2337
12	11.2552	10.5753	9.9539	9.3850	8.8632	8.3838	7.9427	7.6361	7.1607	6.8137	6.4924	6.1944	5.9176	5.6603	5.4206
13	12.1338	11.3483	10.6349	9.9856	9.3935	8.8527	8.3576	7.9038	7.4869	7.1034	6.7499	6.4235	6.1218	5.8424	5.5831
14	13.0038	12.1062	11.2960	10.5631	9.8986	9.2950	8.7454	8.2442	7.7861	7.3667	6.9819	6.6282	6.3025	6.0021	5.7245
15	13.8651	12.8492	11.9379	11.1183	10.3796	9.7122	9.1079	8.5595	8.0607	7.6061	7.1909	6.8109	6.4624	6.1422	5.8474
16	14.7180	13.5777	12.5610	11.6522	10.8377	10.1059	9.4466	8.8514	8.3125	7.8237	7.3792	6.9740	6.6039	6.2651	5.9542
17	15.5624	14.2918	13.1660	12.1656	11.2740	10.4772	9.7632	9.1216	8.5436	8.0215	7.5488	7.1196	6.7291	6.3729	6.0472
18	16.3984	14.9920	13.7534	12.6592	11.6895	10.8276	10.0591	9.3719	8.7556	8.2014	7.7016	7.2497	6.8399	6.4674	6.1280
19	17.2261	15.2684	14.3237	13.1339	12.0853	11.1581	10.3356	9.6036	8.9501	8.3649	7.8393	7.3650	6.9380	6.5504	6.1982
20	18.0457	16.3514	14.8774	13.5903	12.4622	11.4699	10.5940	9.8181	9.1285	8.5136	7.9633	7.4694	7.0248	6.6231	6.2593
21	18.8571	17.0111	15.4149	14.0291	12.8211	11.7640	10.8355	10.0168	9.2922	8.6487	8.0751	7.5620	7.1016	6.6870	6.3125
22	19.6605	17.6581	15.9368	14.4511	13.1630	12.0416	11.0612	10.2007	9.4424	8.7715	8.1757	7.6446	7.1695	6.7429	6.3587
23	20.4559	18.2921	16.4435	14.8568	13.4885	12.3033	11.2722	10.3710	9.5802	8.8832	8.2664	7.7184	7.2297	6.7921	6.3988
24	21.2435	18.9139	16.9355	15.2469	13.7986	12.5503	11.4693	10.5287	9.7066	8.9847	8.3481	7.7843	7.2829	6.8351	6.4338
25	22.0233	19.5234	17.4131	15.6220	14.0939	12.7833	11.6536	10.6748	9.8226	9.0770	8.4217	7.8431	7.3300	6.8729	6.4641

n	16%	17%	18%	19%	20%	21%	22%	23%	24%	25%	26%	27%	28%	29%	30%
1	0.8621	0.8547	0.8475	0.8403	0.8333	0.8264	0.8197	0.8130	0.8065	0.8000	0.7937	0.7874	0.7813	0.7752	0.7692
2	1.6052	1.5852	1.5656	1.5465	1.5278	1.5095	1.4915	1.4740	1.4568	1.4400	1.4235	1.4074	1.3916	1.3761	1.3609
3	2.2459	2.2096	2.1743	2.1399	2.1065	2.0739	2.0422	2.0114	1.9813	1.9520	1.9234	1.8956	1.8684	1.8420	1.8161
4	2.7982	2.7432	2.6901	2.6386	2.5887	2.5404	2.4936	2.4483	2.4043	2.3616	2.3202	2.2800	2.2410	2.2031	2.1662
5	3.2743	3.1993	3.1272	3.0576	2.9906	2.9260	2.8636	2.8035	2.7454	2.6893	2.6351	2.5827	2.5320	2.4830	2.4356
6	3.6847	3.5892	3.4976	3.4098	3.3255	3.2446	3.1669	3.0923	3.0205	2.9514	2.8850	2.8210	2.7594	2.7000	2.6427
7	4.0386	3.9224	3.8115	3.7057	3.6046	3.5079	3.4155	3.3270	3.2423	3.1611	3.0833	3.0087	2.9370	2.8682	2.8021
8	4.3436	4.2072	4.0776	3.9544	3.8372	3.7256	3.6193	3.5179	3.4212	3.3289	3.2407	3.1564	3.0758	2.9986	2.9247
9	4.6065	4.4506	4.3030	4.1633	4.0310	3.9054	3.7863	3.6731	3.5655	3.4631	3.3657	3.2728	3.1842	3.0997	3.0190
10	4.8332	4.6586	4.4941	4.3389	4.1925	4.0541	3.9232	3.7993	3.6819	3.5705	3.4648	3.3644	3.2689	3.1781	3.0915
11	5.0286	4.8364	4.6560	4.4865	4.3271	4.1769	4.0354	3.9018	3.7757	3.6564	3.5435	3.4365	3.3351	3.2388	3.1473
12	5.1971	4.9884	4.7932	4.6105	4.4392	4.2785	4.1274	3.9852	3.8514	3.7251	3.6060	3.4933	3.3868	3.2850	3.1903
13	5.3423	5.1183	4.9095	4.7147	4.5327	4.3624	4.2028	4.0530	3.9124	3.7801	3.6555	3.5381	3.4272	3.3224	3.2233
14	5.4675	5.2293	5.0081	4.8023	4.6106	4.4317	4.2646	4.1082	3.9616	3.8241	3.6949	3.5733	3.4587	3.3507	3.2487
15	5.5755	5.3242	5.0916	4.8759	4.6755	4.4890	4.3152	4.1530	4.0013	3.8593	3.7261	3.6010	3.4834	3.3726	3.2682
16	5.6685	5.4053	5.1624	4.9377	4.7296	4.5364	4.3567	4.1894	4.0333	3.8874	3.7509	3.6228	3.5026	3.3896	3.2832
17	5.7487	5.4746	5.2223	4.9897	4.7746	4.5755	4.3908	4.2190	4.0591	3.9099	3.7705	3.6400	3.5177	3.4028	3.2948
18	5.8178	5.5339	5.2732	5.0333	4.8122	4.6079	4.4187	4.2431	4.0799	3.9279	3.7861	3.6536	3.5294	3.4130	3.3037
19	5.8775	5.5845	5.3176	5.0700	4.8435	4.6345	4.4415	4.2627	4.0967	3.9424	3.7985	3.6642	3.5386	3.4210	3.3105
20	5.9288	5.6278	5.3527	5.1009	4.8696	4.6567	4.4603	4.2786	4.1103	3.9539	3.8083	3.6726	3.5458	3.4271	3.3158
21	5.9731	5.6648	5.3837	5.1268	4.8913	4.6750	4.4756	4.2916	4.1212	3.9631	3.8161	3.6792	3.5514	3.4319	3.3198
22	6.0113	5.6964	5.4099	5.1486	4.9094	4.6900	4.4882	4.3021	4.1300	3.9705	3.8223	3.6844	3.5558	3.4356	3.3230
23	6.0442	5.7234	5.4321	5.1668	4.9245	4.7025	4.4985	4.3106	4.1371	3.9764	3.8273	3.6885	3.5592	3.4384	3.3254
24	6.0726	5.7465	5.4509	5.1822	4.9371	4.7128	4.5070	4.3176	4.1428	3.9811	3.8312	3.6918	3.5619	3.4406	3.3272
25	6.0971	5.7662	5.4669	5.1951	4.9476	4.7213	4.5139	4.3232	4.1474	3.9849	3.8342	3.6943	3.5640	3.4423	3.3286

Example The present value of $1.00 received per year for the next 25 years, discounted at 10 percent, is $9.07 ($1.00 × 9.0770 = $9.07).

Future Value of an Annuity ($1): $FV_a = PMT \left[\sum_{t=1}^{n} (1+i)^{n-t} \right]$

where $\sum_{t=1}^{n} (1 + i)^{n-t} = FVAIF_{i,n}$ and is shown in the following table.

Period	1%	2%	3%	4%	5%	6%	7%	8%	9%	10%	11%	12%	13%	14%	15%
1	1.000	1.000	1.000	1.000	1.000	1.000	1.000	1.000	1.000	1.000	1.000	1.000	1.000	1.000	1.000
2	2.010	2.020	2.030	2.040	2.050	2.060	2.070	2.080	2.090	2.100	2.110	2.120	2.130	2.140	2.150
3	3.030	3.060	3.091	3.122	3.152	3.184	3.215	3.246	3.278	3.310	3.342	3.374	3.407	3.440	3.472
4	4.060	4.122	4.184	4.246	4.310	4.375	4.440	4.506	4.573	4.641	4.710	4.779	4.850	4.921	4.993
5	5.101	5.204	5.309	5.416	5.526	5.637	5.751	5.867	5.985	6.105	6.228	6.353	6.480	6.610	6.742
6	6.152	6.308	6.468	6.633	6.802	6.975	7.153	7.336	7.523	7.716	7.913	8.115	8.323	8.535	8.754
7	7.214	7.434	7.662	7.898	8.142	8.394	8.654	8.923	9.200	9.487	9.783	10.089	10.405	10.730	11.067
8	8.286	8.583	8.892	9.214	9.549	9.897	10.260	10.637	11.028	11.436	11.859	12.300	12.757	13.233	13.727
9	9.368	9.755	10.159	10.583	11.027	11.491	11.978	12.488	13.021	13.579	14.164	14.776	15.416	16.085	16.786
10	10.462	10.950	11.464	12.006	12.578	13.181	13.816	14.487	15.193	15.937	16.722	17.549	18.420	19.337	20.304
11	11.567	12.169	12.808	13.486	14.207	14.972	15.784	16.645	17.560	18.531	19.561	20.655	21.814	23.044	24.349
12	12.682	13.412	14.192	15.026	15.917	16.870	17.888	18.977	20.141	21.384	22.713	24.133	25.650	27.271	29.001
13	13.809	14.680	15.618	16.627	17.713	18.882	20.141	21.495	22.953	24.523	26.211	28.029	29.984	32.088	34.352
14	14.947	15.974	17.086	18.292	19.598	21.015	22.550	24.215	26.019	27.975	30.095	32.392	34.882	37.581	40.504
15	16.097	17.293	18.599	20.023	21.578	23.276	25.129	27.152	29.361	31.772	34.405	37.280	40.417	43.842	47.580
16	17.258	18.639	20.157	21.824	23.657	25.672	27.888	30.324	33.003	35.949	39.190	42.753	46.671	50.980	55.717
17	18.430	20.012	21.761	23.697	25.840	28.213	30.840	33.750	36.973	40.544	44.500	48.883	53.738	59.117	65.075
18	19.614	21.412	23.414	25.645	28.132	30.905	33.999	37.450	41.301	45.599	50.396	55.749	61.724	68.393	75.836
19	20.811	22.840	25.117	27.671	30.539	33.760	37.379	41.446	46.018	51.158	56.939	63.439	70.748	78.968	88.211
20	22.019	24.297	26.870	29.778	33.066	36.785	40.995	45.762	51.159	57.274	64.202	72.052	80.946	91.024	102.443
21	23.239	25.783	28.676	31.969	35.719	39.992	44.865	50.422	56.764	64.002	72.264	81.698	92.468	104.767	118.809
22	24.471	27.299	30.536	34.248	38.505	43.392	49.005	55.456	62.872	71.402	81.213	92.502	105.489	120.434	137.630
23	25.716	28.845	32.452	36.618	41.430	46.995	53.435	60.893	69.531	79.542	91.147	104.602	120.203	138.295	159.274
24	26.973	30.421	34.426	39.082	44.501	50.815	58.176	66.764	76.789	88.496	102.173	118.154	136.829	158.656	184.166
25	28.243	32.030	36.459	41.645	47.726	54.864	63.248	73.105	84.699	98.346	114.412	133.333	155.616	181.867	212.790

Period	16%	17%	18%	19%	20%	21%	22%	23%	24%	25%	26%	27%	28%	29%	30%
1	1.000	1.000	1.000	1.000	1.000	1.000	1.000	1.000	1.000	1.000	1.000	1.000	1.000	1.000	1.000
2	2.160	2.170	2.180	2.190	2.200	2.210	2.220	2.230	2.240	2.250	2.260	2.270	2.280	2.290	2.300
3	3.506	3.539	3.572	3.606	3.640	3.674	3.708	3.743	3.778	3.813	3.848	3.883	3.918	3.954	3.990
4	5.066	5.141	5.215	5.291	5.368	5.446	5.524	5.604	5.684	5.766	5.848	5.931	6.016	6.101	6.187
5	6.877	7.014	7.154	7.297	7.442	7.589	7.740	7.893	8.048	8.207	8.368	8.533	8.700	8.870	9.043
6	8.977	9.207	9.442	9.683	9.930	10.183	10.442	10.708	10.980	11.259	11.544	11.837	12.136	12.442	12.756
7	11.414	11.772	12.141	12.523	12.916	13.321	13.740	14.171	14.615	15.073	15.546	16.032	16.534	17.051	17.583
8	14.240	14.773	15.327	15.902	16.499	17.119	17.762	18.430	19.123	19.842	20.588	21.361	22.163	22.995	23.858
9	17.518	18.285	19.086	19.923	20.799	21.714	22.670	23.669	24.712	25.802	26.940	28.129	29.369	30.664	32.015
10	21.321	22.393	23.521	24.709	25.959	27.274	28.657	30.113	31.643	33.253	34.945	36.723	38.592	40.556	42.619
11	25.733	27.200	28.755	30.403	32.150	34.001	35.962	38.039	40.238	42.566	45.030	47.639	50.398	53.318	56.405
12	30.850	32.824	34.931	37.180	39.580	42.141	44.873	47.787	50.895	54.208	57.738	61.501	65.510	69.780	74.326
13	36.786	39.404	42.218	45.244	48.496	51.991	55.745	59.778	64.109	68.760	73.750	79.106	84.853	91.016	97.624
14	43.672	47.102	50.818	54.841	59.196	63.909	69.009	74.528	80.496	86.949	93.925	101.465	109.611	118.411	127.912
15	51.659	56.109	60.965	66.260	72.035	78.330	85.191	92.669	100.815	109.687	119.346	129.860	141.302	153.750	167.285
16	60.925	66.648	72.938	79.850	87.442	95.779	104.933	114.983	126.010	138.109	151.375	165.922	181.867	199.337	218.470
17	71.673	78.978	87.067	96.021	105.930	116.892	129.019	142.428	157.252	173.636	191.733	211.721	233.790	258.145	285.011
18	84.140	93.404	103.739	115.265	128.116	142.439	158.403	176.187	195.993	218.045	242.583	269.885	300.250	334.006	371.514
19	98.603	110.283	123.412	138.165	154.739	173.351	194.251	217.710	244.031	273.556	306.654	343.754	385.321	431.868	483.968
20	115.379	130.031	146.626	165.417	186.687	210.755	237.986	268.783	303.598	342.945	387.384	437.568	494.210	558.110	630.157
21	134.840	153.136	174.019	197.846	225.024	256.013	291.343	331.603	377.461	429.681	489.104	556.710	633.589	720.962	820.204
22	157.414	180.169	206.342	236.436	271.028	310.775	356.438	408.871	469.052	538.101	617.270	708.022	811.993	931.040	1067.265
23	183.600	211.798	244.483	282.359	326.234	377.038	435.854	503.911	582.624	673.626	778.760	900.187	1040.351	1202.042	1388.443
24	213.976	248.803	289.490	337.007	392.480	457.215	532.741	620.810	723.453	843.032	982.237	1144.237	1332.649	1551.634	1805.975
25	249.212	292.099	342.598	402.038	471.976	554.230	650.944	764.596	898.038	1054.791	1238.617	1454.180	1706.790	2002.608	2348.765

Example The future value of $1.00 per year for the next 25 years, compounded at 10 percent is $98.35. ($1.00 × 98.346 = $98.35).

163

Future Value of One Dollar: $FV_n = PV_0 (1 + i)^n$

where $(1 + i)^n = FVIF_{i,n}$ and is shown in the following table.

n	1%	2%	3%	4%	5%	6%	7%	8%	9%	10%	11%	12%	13%	14%	15%
1	1.0100	1.0200	1.0300	1.0400	1.0500	1.0600	1.0700	1.0800	1.0900	1.1000	1.1100	1.1200	1.1300	1.1400	1.1500
2	1.0201	1.0404	1.0609	1.0816	1.1025	1.1236	1.1449	1.1664	1.1881	1.2100	1.2321	1.2544	1.2769	1.2996	1.3225
3	1.0303	1.0612	1.0927	1.1249	1.1576	1.1910	1.2250	1.2597	1.2950	1.3310	1.3676	1.4049	1.4429	1.4815	1.5209
4	1.0406	1.0824	1.1255	1.1699	1.2155	1.2625	1.3108	1.3605	1.4116	1.4641	1.5181	1.5735	1.6305	1.6890	1.7490
5	1.0510	1.1041	1.1593	1.2167	1.2763	1.3382	1.4026	1.4693	1.5386	1.6105	1.6851	1.7623	1.8424	1.9254	2.0114
6	1.0615	1.1261	1.1941	1.2653	1.3401	1.4185	1.5007	1.5869	1.6771	1.7716	1.8704	1.9738	2.0820	2.1950	2.3131
7	1.0721	1.1487	1.2299	1.3159	1.4071	1.5036	1.6058	1.7138	1.8280	1.9487	2.0762	2.2107	2.3526	2.5023	2.6600
8	1.0829	1.1717	1.2668	1.3686	1.4775	1.5939	1.7182	1.8509	1.9926	2.1436	2.3045	2.4760	2.6584	2.8526	3.0590
9	1.0937	1.1951	1.3048	1.4233	1.5513	1.6895	1.8385	1.9990	2.1719	2.3580	2.5580	2.7731	3.0040	3.2520	3.5179
10	1.1046	1.2190	1.3439	1.4802	1.6289	1.7909	1.9672	2.1589	2.3674	2.5937	2.8394	3.1059	3.3946	3.7072	4.0456
11	1.1157	1.2434	1.3842	1.5395	1.7103	1.8983	2.1049	2.3316	2.5804	2.8531	3.1518	3.4786	3.8359	4.2262	4.6524
12	1.1268	1.2682	1.4258	1.6010	1.7959	2.0122	2.2522	2.5182	2.8127	3.1384	3.4985	3.8960	4.3345	4.8179	5.3503
13	1.1381	1.2936	1.4685	1.6651	1.8857	2.1329	2.4098	2.7196	3.0658	3.4523	3.8833	4.3635	4.8980	5.4924	6.1528
14	1.1495	1.3195	1.5126	1.7317	1.9799	2.2609	2.5785	2.9372	3.3417	3.7975	4.3104	4.8871	5.5348	6.2616	7.0757
15	1.1610	1.3459	1.5580	1.8009	2.0789	2.3966	2.7590	3.1722	3.6425	4.1773	4.7846	5.4736	6.2543	7.1379	8.1371
16	1.1726	1.3728	1.6047	1.8730	2.1829	2.5404	2.9522	3.4259	3.9703	4.5950	5.3109	6.1304	7.0673	8.1373	9.3576
17	1.1843	1.4002	1.6529	1.9479	2.2920	2.6928	3.1588	3.7000	4.3276	5.0545	5.8951	6.8660	7.9861	9.2765	10.761
18	1.1962	1.4283	1.7024	2.0258	2.4066	2.8543	3.3799	3.9960	4.7171	5.5599	6.5436	7.6900	9.0243	10.575	12.376
19	1.2081	1.4568	1.7535	2.1069	2.5270	3.0256	3.6165	4.3157	5.1417	6.1159	7.2633	8.6128	10.107	12.056	14.232
20	1.2202	1.4860	1.8061	2.1911	2.6533	3.2071	3.8697	4.6610	5.6044	6.7275	8.0623	9.6463	11.523	13.744	16.367
21	1.2324	1.5157	1.8603	2.2788	2.7860	3.3996	4.1406	5.0038	6.1088	7.4003	8.9492	10.804	13.021	15.668	18.822
22	1.2447	1.5460	1.9161	2.3699	2.9253	3.6035	4.4304	5.4365	6.6586	8.1403	9.9336	12.100	14.714	17.861	21.645
23	1.2572	1.5769	1.9736	2.4647	3.0715	3.8198	4.7405	5.8714	7.2579	8.9543	11.026	13.552	16.627	20.362	24.892
24	1.2697	1.6084	2.0328	2.5633	3.2251	4.0489	5.0724	6.3412	7.9111	9.8497	12.239	15.179	18.788	23.212	28.625
25	1.2824	1.6406	2.0937	2.6658	3.3864	4.2919	5.4274	6.8485	8.6231	10.835	13.586	17.000	21.231	26.462	32.919

n	16%	17%	18%	19%	20%	21%	22%	23%	24%	25%	26%	27%	28%	29%	30%
1	1.1600	1.1700	1.1800	1.1900	1.2000	1.2100	1.2200	1.2300	1.2400	1.2500	1.2600	1.2700	1.2800	1.2900	1.3000
2	1.3456	1.3689	1.3924	1.4161	1.4400	1.4641	1.4884	1.5129	1.5376	1.5625	1.5876	1.6129	1.6384	1.6641	1.6900
3	1.5609	1.6016	1.6430	1.6852	1.7280	1.7716	1.8159	1.8609	1.9066	1.9531	2.0004	2.0484	2.0972	2.1467	2.1970
4	1.8106	1.8739	1.9388	2.0053	2.0736	2.1436	2.2153	2.2889	2.3642	2.4414	2.5205	2.6015	2.6844	2.7692	2.8561
5	2.1003	2.1925	2.2878	2.3864	2.4883	2.5937	2.7027	2.8153	2.9316	3.0518	3.1758	3.3038	3.4360	3.5723	3.7129
6	2.4364	2.5652	2.6996	2.8398	2.9860	3.1384	3.2973	3.4628	3.6352	3.8147	4.0015	4.1959	4.3981	4.6083	4.8268
7	2.8262	3.0012	3.1855	3.3793	3.5832	3.7975	4.0227	4.2593	4.5077	4.7684	5.0419	5.3288	5.6295	5.9447	6.2749
8	3.2784	3.5115	3.7589	4.0214	4.2998	4.5950	4.9077	5.2389	5.5895	5.9605	6.3528	6.7675	7.2058	7.6686	8.1573
9	3.8030	4.1084	4.4355	4.7855	5.1598	5.5599	5.9874	6.4439	6.9310	7.4506	8.0045	8.5948	9.2234	9.8925	10.605
10	4.4114	4.8068	5.2338	5.6947	6.1917	6.7275	7.3046	7.9260	8.5944	9.3132	10.086	10.915	11.806	12.761	13.786
11	5.1173	5.6240	6.1759	6.7767	7.4301	8.1403	8.9117	9.7489	10.657	11.642	12.708	13.863	15.112	16.462	17.922
12	5.9360	6.5801	7.2876	8.0642	8.9161	9.8497	10.872	11.991	13.215	14.552	16.012	17.605	19.343	21.237	23.298
13	6.8858	7.6987	8.5994	9.5965	10.699	11.918	13.264	14.749	16.386	18.190	20.175	22.359	24.759	27.395	30.288
14	7.9875	9.0075	10.147	11.420	12.839	14.421	16.182	18.141	20.319	22.737	25.421	28.396	31.691	35.339	39.374
15	9.2655	10.539	11.974	13.590	15.407	17.449	19.742	22.314	25.196	28.422	32.030	36.063	40.565	45.588	51.186
16	10.748	12.330	14.129	16.172	18.488	21.114	24.086	27.446	31.243	35.527	40.358	45.799	51.923	58.898	66.542
17	12.468	14.427	16.672	19.244	22.186	25.548	29.384	33.759	38.741	44.409	50.851	58.165	66.461	75.862	86.504
18	14.463	16.879	19.673	22.901	26.623	30.913	35.849	41.523	48.039	55.511	64.072	73.870	85.071	97.862	112.46
19	16.777	19.748	23.214	27.252	31.948	37.404	43.736	51.074	59.568	69.389	80.731	93.815	108.89	126.24	146.19
20	19.461	23.106	27.393	32.429	38.338	45.259	53.358	62.821	73.864	86.736	101.72	119.15	139.38	162.85	190.05
21	22.575	27.034	32.324	38.591	46.005	54.764	65.096	77.269	91.592	108.42	128.17	151.31	178.41	210.08	247.07
22	26.186	31.629	38.142	45.923	55.206	66.264	79.418	95.041	113.57	135.53	161.49	192.17	228.36	271.00	321.18
23	30.376	37.006	45.008	54.649	66.247	80.180	96.889	116.90	140.83	169.41	203.48	244.05	292.30	349.59	417.54
24	35.236	43.297	53.109	65.032	79.497	97.017	118.21	143.79	174.63	211.76	256.39	309.95	374.14	450.98	542.80
25	40.874	50.658	62.669	77.388	95.396	117.39	144.21	176.86	216.54	264.70	323.05	393.63	478.91	581.76	705.64

Example The future value of $1.00 compounded at 10 percent for 10 years is $2.59 ($1.00 × 2.5937 = $2.59).

Appendix 6

Four-Place Common Logarithms

COMMON LOGARITHMS

x	0	1	2	3	4	5	6	7	8	9
1.0	.0000	.0043	.0086	.0128	.0170	.0212	.0253	.0294	.0334	.0374
1.1	.0414	.0453	.0492	.0531	.0569	.0607	.0645	.0682	.0719	.0755
1.2	.0792	.0828	.0864	.0899	.0934	.0969	.1004	.1038	.1072	.1106
1.3	.1139	.1173	.1206	.1239	.1271	.1303	.1355	.1367	.1399	.1430
1.4	.1461	.1492	.1523	.1553	.1584	.1614	.1644	.1673	.1703	.1732
1.5	.1761	.1790	.1818	.1847	.1875	.1903	.1931	.1959	.1987	.2014
1.6	.2041	.2068	.2095	.2122	.2148	.2175	.2201	.2227	.2253	.2279
1.7	.2304	.2330	.2355	.2380	.2405	.2430	.2455	.2480	.2504	.2529
1.8	.2553	.2577	.2601	.2625	.2648	.2672	.2695	.2718	.2742	.2765
1.9	.2788	.2810	.2833	.2856	.2878	.2900	.2923	.2945	.2967	.2989
2.0	.3010	.3032	.3054	.3075	.3096	.3118	.3139	.3160	.3181	.3201
2.1	.3222	.3243	.3263	.3284	.3304	.3324	.3345	.3365	.3385	.3404
2.2	.3424	.3444	.3464	.3483	.3502	.3522	.3541	.3560	.3579	.3598
2.3	.3617	.3636	.3655	.3674	.3692	.3711	.3729	.3747	.3766	.3784
2.4	.3802	.3820	.3838	.3856	.3874	.3892	.3909	.3927	.3945	.3962
2.5	.3979	.3997	.4014	.4031	.4048	.4065	.4082	.4099	.4116	.4133
2.6	.4150	.4166	.4183	.4200	.4216	.4232	.4249	.4265	.4281	.4298
2.7	.4314	.4330	.4346	.4362	.4378	.4393	.4409	.4425	.4440	.4456
2.8	.4472	.4487	.4502	.4518	.4533	.4548	.4564	.4579	.4594	.4609
2.9	.4624	.4639	.4654	.4669	.4683	.4698	.4713	.4728	.4742	.4757
3.0	.4771	.4786	.4800	.4814	.4829	.4843	.4857	.4871	.4886	.4900
3.1	.4914	.4928	.4942	.4955	.4969	.4983	.4997	.5011	.5024	.5038
3.2	.5051	.5065	.5079	.5092	.5105	.5119	.5132	.5145	.5159	.5172
3.3	.5185	.5198	.5211	.5224	.5237	.5250	.5263	.5276	.5289	.5307
3.4	.5315	.5328	.5340	.5353	.5366	.5378	.5391	.5403	.5416	.5428
3.5	.5441	.5453	.5465	.5478	.5490	.5502	.5514	.5527	.5539	.5551
3.6	.5563	.5575	.5587	.5599	.5611	.5623	.5635	.5647	.5658	.5670
3.7	.5682	.5694	.5705	.5717	.5729	.5740	.5752	.5763	.5775	.5786
3.8	.5798	.5809	.5821	.5832	.5843	.5855	.5866	.5877	.5888	.5899
3.9	.5911	.5922	.5933	.5944	.5955	.5966	.5977	.5988	.5999	.6010
4.0	.6021	.6031	.6042	.6053	.6064	.6075	.6085	.6096	.6107	.6117
4.1	.6128	.6138	.6149	.6160	.6170	.6180	.6191	.6201	.6212	.6222
4.2	.6232	.6243	.6253	.6263	.6274	.6284	.6294	.6304	.6314	.6325
4.3	.6335	.6345	.6355	.6365	.6375	.6385	.6395	.6405	.6415	.6425
4.4	.6435	.6444	.6454	.6464	.6474	.6484	.6493	.6503	.6513	.6522
4.5	.6532	.6542	.6551	.6561	.6571	.6580	.6590	.6599	.6609	.6618
4.6	.6628	.6637	.6646	.6656	.6665	.6675	.6684	.6693	.6702	.6712
4.7	.6721	.6730	.6739	.6749	.6758	.6767	.6776	.6785	.6794	.6803
4.8	.6812	.6821	.6830	.6839	.6848	.6857	.6866	.6875	.6884	.6893
4.9	.6902	.6911	.6920	.6928	.6937	.6946	.6955	.6964	.6972	.6981
5.0	.6990	.6998	.7007	.7016	.7024	.7033	.7042	.7050	.7059	.7067
5.1	.7076	.7084	.7093	.7101	.7110	.7118	.7126	.7135	.7143	.7152
5.2	.7160	.7168	.7177	.7185	.7193	.7202	.7210	.7218	.7226	.7235
5.3	.7243	.7251	.7259	.7267	.7275	.7284	.7292	.7300	.7308	.7316
5.4	.7324	.7332	.7340	.7348	.7356	.7364	.7372	.7380	.7388	.7396

x	0	1	2	3	4	5	6	7	8	9
5.5	.7404	.7412	.7419	.7427	.7435	.7443	.7451	.7459	.7466	.7474
5.6	.7482	.7490	.7497	.7505	.7513	.7520	.7528	.7536	.7543	.7551
5.7	.7559	.7566	.7574	.7582	.7589	.7597	.7604	.7612	.7619	.7627
5.8	.7634	.7642	.7649	.7657	.7664	.7672	.7679	.7686	.7694	.7701
5.9	.7709	.7716	.7723	.7731	.7738	.7745	.7752	.7760	.7767	.7774
6.0	.7782	.7789	.7796	.7803	.7810	.7818	.7825	.7832	.7839	.7846
6.1	.7853	.7860	.7868	.7875	.7882	.7889	.7896	.7903	.7910	.7917
6.2	.7924	.7931	.7938	.7945	.7952	.7959	.7966	.7973	.7980	.7987
6.3	.7993	.8000	.8007	.8014	.8021	.8028	.8035	.8041	.8048	.8055
6.4	.8062	.8069	.8075	.8082	.8089	.8096	.8102	.8109	.8116	.8122
6.5	.8129	.8136	.8142	.8149	.8156	.8162	.8169	.8176	.8182	.8189
6.6	.8195	.8202	.8209	.8215	.8222	.8228	.8235	.8241	.8248	.8254
6.7	.8261	.8267	.8274	.8280	.8287	.8293	.8299	.8306	.8312	.8319
6.8	.8325	.8331	.8338	.8344	.8351	.8357	.8363	.8370	.8376	.8382
6.9	.8388	.8395	.8401	.8407	.8414	.8420	.8426	.8432	.8439	.8445
7.0	.8451	.8457	.8463	.8470	.8476	.8482	.8488	.8494	.8500	.8506
7.1	.8513	.8519	.8525	.8531	.8537	.8543	.8549	.8555	.8561	.8567
7.2	.8573	.8579	.8585	.8591	.8597	.8603	.8609	.8615	.8621	.8627
7.3	.8633	.8639	.8645	.8651	.8657	.8663	.8669	.8675	.8681	.8686
7.4	.8692	.8698	.8704	.8710	.8716	.8722	.8727	.8733	.8739	.8745
7.5	.8751	.8756	.8762	.8768	.8774	.8779	.8785	.8791	.8797	.8802
7.6	.8808	.8814	.8820	.8825	.8831	.8837	.8842	.8848	.8854	.8859
7.7	.8865	.8871	.8876	.8882	.8887	.8893	.8899	.8904	.8910	.8915
7.8	.8921	.8927	.8932	.8938	.8943	.8949	.8954	.8960	.8965	.8971
7.9	.8976	.8982	.8987	.8993	.8998	.9004	.9009	.9015	.9020	.9025
8.0	.9031	.9036	.9042	.9047	.9053	.9058	.9063	.9069	.9074	.9079
8.1	.9085	.9090	.9096	.9101	.9106	.9112	.9117	.9122	.9128	.9133
8.2	.9138	.9143	.9149	.9154	.9159	.9165	.9170	.9175	.9180	.9186
8.3	.9191	.9196	.9201	.9206	.9212	.9217	.9222	.9227	.9232	.9238
8.4	.9243	.9248	.9253	.9258	.9263	.9269	.9274	.9279	.9284	.9289
8.5	.9294	.9299	.9304	.9309	.9315	.9320	.9325	.9330	.9335	.9340
8.6	.9345	.9350	.9355	.9360	.9365	.9370	.9375	.9380	.9385	.9390
8.7	.9395	.9400	.9405	.9410	.9415	.9420	.9425	.9430	.9435	.9440
8.8	.9445	.9450	.9455	.9460	.9465	.9469	.9474	.9479	.9484	.9489
8.9	.9494	.9499	.9504	.9509	.9513	.9518	.9523	.9528	.9533	.9538
9.0	.9542	.9547	.9552	.9557	.9562	.9566	.9571	.9576	.9581	.9586
9.1	.9590	.9595	.9600	.9605	.9609	.9614	.9619	.9624	.9628	.9633
9.2	.9638	.9643	.9647	.9652	.9657	.9661	.9666	.9671	.9675	.9680
9.3	.9685	.9689	.9694	.9699	.9703	.9708	.9713	.9717	.9722	.9727
9.4	.9731	.9736	.9741	.9745	.9750	.9754	.9759	.9763	.9768	.9773
9.5	.9777	.9782	.9786	.9791	.9795	.9800	.9805	.9809	.9814	.9818
9.6	.9823	.9827	.9832	.9836	.9841	.9845	.9850	.9854	.9859	.9863
9.7	.9868	.9872	.9877	.9881	.9886	.9890	.9894	.9899	.9903	.9908
9.8	.9912	.9917	.9921	.9926	.9930	.9934	.9939	.9943	.9948	.9952
9.9	.9956	.9961	.9965	.9969	.9974	.9978	.9983	.9987	.9991	.9996

169

Index